UNSHRINKABLE

UNSHRINKABLE

Why Strong Women Secretly Criticize, Diminish, and Thwart Themselves... and How to Stop

DARBY BONOMI, PhD

Cheval Press

www.darbybonomi.com

UNSHRINKABLE
Why Strong Women Secretly Criticize, Diminish, and Thwart Themselves...and How to Stop
First Edition

Cover and interior design: JVDW Designs

ISBN 978-1-967509-11-9 *Hardcover*
978-1-967509-10-2 *Paperback*
978-1-967509-09-6 *eBook*
978-1-967509-12-6 *Audiobook*

LCCN 2025926040

For Peter, Adele, and Clara

May you passionately pursue all of your life's adventures secure in the knowledge that you are more than enough and that your mama loves you.

"Courage is being scared to death
but saddling up anyway."

—JOHN WAYNE

"We're not shrink-to-fit."

—DR. DARBY BONOMI

CONTENTS

INTRODUCTION

CHOOSING YOUR OWN PATH

When you've lived long enough, and ridden horses long enough, you learn that life doesn't wait for the perfect moment. Grief doesn't ask if it's a good time. Illness doesn't check your calendar. Horses don't care if you've had a sleepless night, and the judges won't wait because you're carrying something heavy inside.

Right as I began working on this book, I received news no one ever wants to hear: My husband was diagnosed with cancer. The prognosis is good, and we have great care, but we're bracing for a long, winding road. It will take time and stamina from both of us, and yet, I knew I wanted to keep writing. Not because it's easy, but because for me, continuing is my form of coping.

This is how I move through hardship. I show up, stand tall, and carry on. I ride forward, even when the footing isn't ideal.

When my sister died suddenly years ago, I was in shock. She passed away overseas, in Germany. I remember feeling overwhelmed with disbelief, asking myself, "What do I do?" And the answer came, simply: *Go to work.* And I did. I wasn't trying to avoid grief, but there was nothing else I could do. Continuing forward was the only option.

Not everyone understood. One of my patients found out and responded with sharp criticism. In the world of psychoanalysis, some patients can be brutally honest. They test boundaries and push, but that's part of the work. When the patient tore into me, it was painful to hear, but I knew I had made the right choice for me—and for her.

Maybe those sessions weren't the most brilliant of my career, but I was there. I was present, doing the best I could while carrying some raw and real emotions of my own. I was holding space for someone else while managing my own heartbreak—staying upright in the saddle, if you will, even though the temptation to collapse was sometimes strong.

Through experiences like that, I've learned something about myself: I'm resilient. I don't shrink, even when I'd like to. I'm good at showing up for myself and the people I love. More importantly, I've learned not to apologize for it. For some of us, movement is medicine, and work is stabilizing. When life gets hard, as it inevitably will, carrying on doesn't mean you're denying the pain. It means you're giving yourself permission to move *with* it rather than be diminished *by* it.

I'm not telling you this for sympathy. I'm sharing my story because this book, and your journey through it, is not happening in a vacuum. Just like you, I'm living real life while trying to grow, lead, and ride through it. Just like you, some days, I'm firing on all cylinders. Other days, I might be a little less energetic. But I'll be here, riding on, because when everything in me wants to shrink, sometimes the most meaningful thing I can do is saddle up anyway. I hope, as you go through these pages, that you find inspiration and guidance to do the same.

There's No One Right Way to Ride This Life

One of the most powerful lessons I've learned, on horseback and off, is that honoring your own truth isn't always easy, but you have to do it anyway. This truth is *so* important. In fact, it's an essential focus of this book.

When my sister died, I chose to go to work not because I was numbing myself or trying to prove something, but because that was the right path for me. It gave me purpose when everything else felt uncertain. For someone else, that might have looked like avoidance. For me, it was an act of staying present in my own life. I knew what I needed and I honored that, despite the pain, and despite what others said.

In life, as in riding, the moment you begin to move with intention and fullness, someone will have an opinion. This is especially true for women. You'll be too bold or not bold enough. Too strong or too soft. Too focused on your goals, or not ambitious enough. The same is true in motherhood, in business, and in the saddle.

Choose to work full time with three kids? You'll be criticized. Choose to stay home and focus on family? You'll be criticized. Choose to ride competitively after you have a baby, or invest in your own development while others think you should be focused elsewhere? You'll hear about it.

But the truth is *there's no one right way*. There is only what works for each of us, individually. This is where we, as women, can do better. We need to stop assuming that what's right for one of us is right for all of us. We need to support each other's choices, even when they differ from our own. You don't need to justify the way you show up in your life or your work. You only need to be in touch with what's real and necessary for *you*.

If I've learned anything through decades of psychology, motherhood, marriage, riding, and coaching, it's that *when a woman finally begins to show up fully and authentically in her own life, great things blossom.*

I want this book to help you start to stand in *your* full authentic self. To stop secretly thwarting your own desires. To silence the inner critic. To resist the pull to shrink. I'll share some of my story—both my struggles and my successes—with you. I'll share stories of my patients' and clients' challenges and triumphs. My hope is that by doing so, you'll be able to see what's possible for your own life, no matter what you're going through. Finally, I'll share a trail map to help you play bigger in your own life—to claim your voice, embrace your authenticity, and show up as fully and brightly as you desire. To become *unshrinkable.*

As you read through the following pages, remember: You decide what balance looks like. You choose your own path.

I Know This Work

The insights in these pages aren't only personal reflections. They're reflections grounded in my many years of training and experience treating and coaching hundreds of women over the past thirty-five years.

Early in my career, I was a clinical psychologist and psychoanalyst in private practice in San Francisco. I worked with adult and adolescent patients, mostly women, who suffered mainly from anxiety and depression. They were stuck in their lives in one form or another, and I helped them see and overcome the obstacles that were interfering with living more freely and happily. In addition, I spent considerable time teaching and mentoring young clinicians. I was on the faculty at the San Francisco Center for Psychoanalysis and was a clinical supervisor at many of the hospitals in San Francisco. As my career developed, I specialized in working with and mentoring young women and mothers. I always had an interest in adult development, having conducted my doctoral research on creativity and the adult life cycle. To this day, I still bring a developmental perspective to every client I work with.

For the past ten years, my practice has shifted to sport and performance coaching. I work mainly with amateur and professional athletes, mostly equestrians (like myself), along with entrepreneurs and young professionals starting their businesses. Almost all of my clients are women, and all of them aim to play bigger in their lives. They do not want to shrink under their own self-criticism or that of others, or their belief that somehow they are not enough. My clients, who range in age from ten to seventy, are similar. They are driven, perfectionistic, hardworking, and brilliant—and all of them suffer from self-doubt and, usually, people-pleasing. They come to me wanting guidance, support, and clarity. They get all of that, along with help in becoming crystal clear and unapologetic about their goals *and* determining a road map to get where they want to go. I keep them accountable, noticing those times when they inadvertently diminish themselves in one way or another, and get them back on their intended track.

This book is part memoir and part trail map—a way for me to guide you in creating real change in your life. It's based on my life experience, but more importantly, it's based on my professional experience of treating and working with thousands of women who struggle with showing up in the world fully, authentically, and *powerfully* themselves. I aim to get you to actively think about your own internal beliefs about yourself, and then to *change those thoughts and the behaviors that follow*. I know, after years of this work, that if you do, you'll feel different. You'll be better equipped to move past your obstacles. Most of all, you'll become unshrinkable.

To achieve this, I've divided the book into three sections. Part 1 takes you through parts of my own story. I offer it as a way to show you that I *see* you, because I have been there too. Part 2 examines the many ways that I've seen women—both myself and my clients—play small. I hope you will see parts of yourself reflected in those stories, because I want you to know that you are not alone in this journey. Finally, Part 3 is a trail map that lays out concrete, actionable ways to move beyond brittleness and fear and live the life you aspire to and that aligns with your big goals.

Let's do this.

PART I

YOU AND ME

ONE

HOW I GOT HERE

IN EVERY WOMAN'S STORY, THERE ARE EARLY CHAPters that shape how she shows up later in other areas of life: the boardroom, the barn, her relationships. For me, those chapters began in a household filled with contradictions. I grew up trying to make sense of a world that didn't make a lot of sense.

My mother was brilliant. An accomplished academic and a perfectionist, she went to the University of Michigan at a time when that was no small feat for a woman. She had ambition, drive, and a vision for her life that didn't include children. I was not planned. To be honest, she never really envisioned herself as a mother. My sister (ten years my junior) and I came to understand that early on. My mother was capable of deep intellectual engagement, but emotionally, she was distant and sometimes absent entirely.

When I was six months old, my mother left my father and moved in with her parents. Then, when I was about two and a half, she moved again, this time to California, to live with a former boyfriend. But he didn't want another man's child around. So she told my father, whom I didn't really know at the time, "You have to come get her." And he did. Just like that, I was handed off, and I went to live with my dad.

Eventually, after six years or so, my mother and father got back together, at least for a while. Those formative years were marked by instability, inconsistency, and emotional uncertainty. There were long stretches when I barely saw my mom, and when she returned, she wasn't alone. She came back with a baby boy, my half brother. I was no longer the only child in the story, and I felt it. In fact, I felt replaced.

That sense of being upstaged, of suddenly becoming less important, shaped my development in ways I've had to unpack slowly and deliberately over the years. It planted a fear that I could be pushed aside if someone better, smarter, or more lovable came along. In my case, it was a boy, and that gender piece mattered too. It layered on questions about whether being a girl, even a good one, was enough.

So I did what many girls in uncertain homes do: I made myself the "perfect little girl." Or at least, I tried. I figured if I followed every rule, got straight As, never made waves, and kept my emotions in check, I'd be safe, loved, and needed. I tried to earn my place in a family that felt like it was always on the verge of moving out from under me.

I know now that trying to be perfect doesn't protect you from loss, but still, it does give you something to control. And control can feel a lot like safety when everything else is uncertain.

When I was ten years old, my sister was born. By the time I was eighteen, my parents had separated, and when I was nineteen, they divorced again. The family dynamics only grew more complex from there. I've done enough work (two full psychoanalyses, in fact) to understand how deeply those early years carved tracks in my psyche. However, those same tracks, painful as they were, led me to the work I do now—and it's work I wouldn't trade for the world. My past experiences gave me empathy, insight, and the fire to understand human behavior, especially my own.

Looking back now, I can see how many mixed messages I received about women and worth. My mother, for all her intellect and ambition, gave up a life she had wanted in order to follow a man and become a mother, even though she didn't want to be. I was the evidence of that trade-off, and that left a mark.

Those contradictions helped me understand that wholeness doesn't come from fitting into someone else's idea of what we should be. It comes from figuring out what we need to be for ourselves and riding toward that, no matter who questions us.

Mixed Messages and the Mother Wound

In our house, there were always two sets of rules—one for boys, and one for girls. It wasn't stated outright, but it was unmistakable. My half brother had a different playbook. He didn't have to do chores and was constantly given special treatment. My sister Megan and I both felt it. We talked about it often. The injustice wasn't subtle, and it affected the way we understood gender and what was expected of us as girls.

However, the message was confusing because my mother *said* all the right things. She was highly intelligent—a passionate feminist who went back to law school later in life. She marched for women's rights and spoke boldly about independence and equality. She told me to stand on my own two feet, to be strong and self-reliant, to never settle.

That was the external narrative: Women are powerful and should claim their place in the world. But what she modeled in our home was something else entirely.

The roles in our family didn't reflect her ideals, and with me, in particular, there was a tension she couldn't seem to resolve. I've come to believe that on some level, she both admired my strength *and* feared it. She didn't know what to do with a daughter who was powerful in ways she hadn't been able to be. She was proud of me, but also felt threatened. Supportive, yet sometimes cruel.

It's hard to admit that about your mother, especially when everyone outside the family saw a different version of her. To the world, she was loving and nurturing. She rescued stray animals and lost people—anyone who needed help, she would show up for them. She gave generously her time, energy, and sometimes money to needy friends and acquaintances alike, but with me, it was more complicated.

With me, she could be withholding and, at times, mean. She was often cutting in a way that nobody else saw. One moment she would encourage me, the next she would tear me down. It wasn't consistent, and it wasn't something I could prepare for. There was no map for navigating her, and maybe that's why I've spent so much of my adult life trying to solve the riddle of who she really was, and what I was supposed to learn from her.

Despite that, I still identified with her. I took on her insecurities—I remember thinking I wasn't very smart or very attractive—and spent my time trying to fill her up, to bolster her image of herself. Finally, though, in the absence of the mothering I needed, I learned to mother myself. I still vividly remember being in my twenties, looking at pictures of myself and thinking, "My body is fine just as it is. Actually, I'm pretty attractive." It was a moment of breaking with her—with her insecurities and the messages she had been sending me (and herself) my whole life.

That was a large part of the tension between us: I rejected her diminished self-worth—her self-identity—and she envied me for it. When I went out into the world, that break continued. Different people, from professors to colleagues to friends, reflected images of myself back to me. They saw me as smart, as engaging, as attractive, as competent. It was eye-opening, because it was validation from people I thought of as mentors that I was enough.

I have compassion for my mother now. If she had felt full and secure in her own right, she would have had the capacity to be proud of me. She wouldn't have felt envy; instead, she would have been able to let the love that I know she felt for me flow through, fully and consistently. But she was beaten down—emotionally, not physically—by her father and by my father, and that informed how she showed up with me.

I was thirteen or fourteen when I made a decision: I would never have a relationship like the one she and my father had. And when I became a mother, especially to my daughters, I made a conscious decision to parent them differently than my parents did with me. I was determined not to pass on that same confusion. My girls know where they stand with me. They know I believe in them. They know I support them, fiercely and without question. I encourage them to be strong, to lead, to take up space, and I back that with unwavering love.

Breaking that cycle and becoming the mother I am to my kids is my greatest achievement in life. And now, I'm here to tell you that *cycles can be broken.* No matter what negative stories you were told—consciously or not—and even if you grew up in a world of mixed messages, you can create clarity in your own home. You can become the mother, the woman, the leader that no one ever modeled for you, and in doing so, you won't just raise confident daughters—you will create more fullness in your own life as you reclaim yourself.

This is true beyond parenting as well. Many women have a tendency to envy others when they do well.

When we envy others, we diminish ourselves. Reveling in other people's ability to live authentically and play big in their own lives multiplies our own joy in living authentically.

Learn from others' successes. Admire them. Champion them. And mentor them.

There was a time, before I ever held my children, that I was deeply afraid I wouldn't be able to love them the way they deserved. The fear was quiet, tucked away in the unconscious corners of my heart and mind, but it was there. I didn't have my first child—my son Peter—until I was thirty-six. Before he was born, I was afraid of becoming a mother. When I found out I was pregnant, something fearful stirred in me. I was in psychoanalysis at the time, and I remember the feeling creeping up like a shadow: *What if I'm just like my own mother?*

When my son was born, I knew immediately that fear wasn't justified. But when I became pregnant a second time, with a girl, the fear surged back: *What if I can't fully love a daughter?*

Maybe it was because I knew too intimately what it felt like to be a daughter who didn't feel fully loved. My mother showed tenderness, but her love was mixed with envy, inconsistency, emotional distance, and abandonment. So now, staring into the unknown of mothering a daughter of my own, I found myself terrified that I would repeat the cycle.

Then Adele was born, and all my fear evaporated in an instant. I looked at this perfect, brilliant, radiant little being, and I was overwhelmed with protective, adoring, joyful love.

There was no envy or comparison, just reverence, and that same love poured out for my second daughter Clara when she was born. My children are beautiful, whip-smart, kindhearted humans, and every time I see them, I feel nothing but awe and pride. I don't envy them. I'm inspired by them.

Mothering them has become one of the truest expressions of who I am, and if I'm honest, it's also a redemption story. I made a conscious decision that I would not repeat what I had lived through. I would be the mother I needed growing up, a mother who stands firm and chooses her children, always.

That's why, looking back, one of the hardest things I've had to come to terms with is the moment my own mother left me behind. When her boyfriend said, "I don't want your ex-husband's baby around," and she chose to send me to my father instead of standing by me, I spent years feeling betrayed. I came to believe that I wasn't worth fighting for. I couldn't understand how a mother could choose a man over her child.

Time and therapy have softened some of those edges, and what I've come to realize is that maybe on some level, she knew she couldn't properly take care of me. Maybe, in her own way, she believed I would be better off with my father. If that's the case, then I believe—now—that she was right. It doesn't erase the pain, but it reframes the decision as an act of strength rather than weakness. A mother who knew her limits made a choice she thought was right for her child, even if it broke something in both of us.

It's taken me decades to find that grace, but that's what this work is really about. We're trying to understand the story we came from and rewrite it where we can, even as we refuse to pass down the parts that hurt us most. In the saddle, in the family, in the self—we get to choose a different way forward. We get to break the cycle. Sometimes, that begins with holding your baby in your arms and saying, "It ends with me."

The Myth of a Charmed Life

People sometimes look at someone like me and assume the road I've traveled has been smooth. I still remember a moment years ago when I was in postgraduate training. A friend casually remarked, "Darby, you lead such a charmed life." I was startled. A charmed life? This was a woman who knew my history, my personal struggles, and those with my family. How could she say that? I felt like she was denying all of the work that I had done so far to lift myself up and propel myself into the profession and life I wanted.

Thirty years later, her words still sting. What she saw on the outside was not the whole package. Surely she saw the polished version: I had enough resources, dressed well, carried myself with confidence, and was doing well financially. From the outside, it looked like I had it all figured out—and I was working on figuring it out—but the truth is, *nobody* leads a charmed life.

Every woman has her story and her struggles, her silent battles and her worries. Just because we don't show our bruises doesn't mean we don't have them. Women like me (and like you) have often clawed our way forward while everyone else assumed we were gliding. We've endured heartache, disappointment, rejection, and grief; navigated impossible decisions; and learned how to keep moving when the ground beneath us gave way.

Behind every "charmed" woman, there's a path no one else sees. In my case, some of that path was walked beside my father. For several of my early, most formative years, it was just him and me, and let me tell you: He was a force to be reckoned with. At six foot three, he was a commanding presence, an antitrust attorney who made his mark in the legal world. He took me in when my mother rejected me and raised me through those early years with a strong presence.

As I got older, however, I found myself needing space from the world in which he loomed so large. I eventually dropped my maiden name, not out of anger or rejection, but because I needed to define myself independent of him. I didn't want to be known only as someone's daughter. I wanted to be myself, so I became Darby Bonomi, instead of Darby Furth.

There's power in naming yourself and deciding who you are, especially when people think they already know you.

My parents came from very different walks of life, but what they had in common was a refusal to accept the limitations handed to them. That determination to rise despite the odds is something I carry in me to this day.

My mother's family was lower-middle class. Her parents, both schoolteachers, left their farming roots in Michigan and were the first in their families to go to college, but the choice to pursue education came at a cost. They were ostracized by their families for leaving the farm and seeking something different. Still, they didn't turn back.

My maternal grandmother, Louise, went on to become a third- and fourth-grade teacher in Grand Haven, Michigan, where she taught for forty-two years. My grandfather taught sixth grade and also had a brief stint as a minor league baseball player before an injury cut that dream short. Education was sacred to them, and that value became deeply ingrained in my mother, who was exceptionally bright and driven. School was her place to shine, and she always did. They lived a good life, though not a wealthy one. Stability came from books and community, not bank accounts.

My father's side of the story was even tougher. He grew up in deep poverty in Harvey, Illinois, a working-class town outside of Chicago that's still struggling to this day. The Depression hit his family hard. His mother was a maid, and his father was a steelworker who lost his job and spiraled into depression. With four children to feed, it was a hard and humbling life.

My grandfather had once dreamed of something different. He'd traveled across the country as a young man, chasing music and adventure, playing saxophone, hoping to somehow hit it big. But then he met Mamie, they fell in love, she got pregnant, and they settled down. He did the right thing. He married her and raised a family, but the weight of life bore down on them.

My dad was the third of four kids, and the only boy. At fourteen, he took a job at the post office, saved his money, and put himself on a path toward something better. He was the kind of man who could move mountains through sheer will. He decided he would go to college, and he did, despite the fact that his parents were furious about it. Believing he was taking resources away from the family, they felt abandoned by him.

That kind of disapproval, coming from your own parents, is a heavy burden, but he didn't let it stop him.

He enrolled at the University of Michigan, where he eventually met my mother. He built a powerful legal career and made (and lost) significant amounts of money. He battled mental illness and wrestled with his own demons, but he always fought. Later in life, despite the pain he had carried, he paid for many things for his own parents, in an attempt at reparation.

When I reflect on all of this, what I find so striking is how the stories of both my parents are the product of the same root challenge. They both had to leave behind the lives they were born into, and in doing so, face the anger and disappointment of the very people who raised them. They had to bet on themselves, even when it meant walking alone. That's a powerful legacy to inherit. As I reflect on who I am, I see how those stories live in me. I am also equipped with the resolve to move forward, and the strength to trust your inner compass, even when others don't understand. The willingness to sacrifice comfort for purpose.

Those aren't just family stories. They're the foundation of the woman I've become. And, they are the reason I believe so deeply in *every* woman's ability to rise, even when the odds are stacked against her.

A Complicated Man

Strength runs in families, but it doesn't always show up the same way. Sometimes it's loud and commanding. Sometimes it's quiet and enduring. In my case, I experienced both.

My dad was a complicated man, but he clearly always loved me. I was just shy of three years old when I went to live with him. At that age, I didn't fully understand what was happening. I didn't really know him yet. My earliest memories from that time are more impressions than detail, but the transition was traumatic, as you might imagine. My mother had moved back to Michigan with her parents, and soon after, my dad took a job at Kellogg because it brought him closer to us.

When my mother eventually left for California, my father followed again. He got a job working for Joseph Alioto, who would later become the mayor of San Francisco. We moved west when I was a little over three years old; I remember the cross-country drive and seeing the Golden Gate Bridge for the first time.

My dad didn't always know what he was doing as a parent. He was no-nonsense, hard-charging, and not particularly warm in the traditional sense, but he was also loyal, passionate, and fiercely protective. He was what people called "a character"—the kind of man you definitely wanted in your corner if you were going to trial. People would often say of him, "Fred is intense, but you want him on your side." And they were right. He could move mountains when he set his mind to something.

He was certainly charismatic. Some people absolutely loved him; he was a charming person. But others despised him because he could be so brutal. He wasn't built for people-pleasing, but he was built for purpose, and in his own way, he was deeply devoted to me. I didn't have his full attention often, though. He worked long hours, but still, I never doubted that I mattered to him. Even when things were tough, I knew I was loved.

People used to ask whether I was okay living with him. "Is she safe with Fred?" they'd say. The concern wasn't completely misplaced. He could be brash and unpredictable, but what they didn't always see was the emotional bond between us. There were plenty of challenges, yes, but my dad gave me something not every little girl gets: a sense of power from a very young age. He respected me, and as I grew older, I was one of the only people in his life who could call him out when it mattered.

There were some moments when I had to stand up to him and tell him no. Those moments weren't easy, but they gave me a kind of confidence that I still possess today. The ability to speak truth to power, even when that power is your own father, is not something you inherit automatically. It's something forged, and my father, for all his flaws and brilliance, helped cultivate it in me.

I carry that strength into every part of my life. I have that strength, in large part, because I was loved—imperfectly but fully—by a man who both expected me to be strong and gave me permission to be.

Why do I share all of this? Because through the course of this book, I want to do the same for you. By sharing my own stories and the stories of some of my clients (identifying details have been changed to protect confidentiality), I hope to show you how you can start to step fully into your own authentic self.

You'll see yourself reflected in these stories, because they deal with the almost-universal struggles we as women go through. But we won't stop there: You'll also see how you can start to mother yourself, to reclaim your voice, and to develop internal and unshakable resilience in any area of your life—and eventually help the women around you start to do the same.

KEY TAKEAWAYS

- No matter what negative stories you were told—consciously or not—or mixed messages you were given, you can create clarity in your own home. You can become the mother, the woman, the leader that no one ever modeled for you, and in doing so, you will create more fullness in your own life as you reclaim yourself.

- One key to playing big in your own life is to learn from others' successes. Admire them. Champion them. Doing so will increase your joy and help you show up fully—and it takes nothing away from you.

TWO

YOU ARE ENOUGH

WHEN I LOOK BACK ON THE START OF MY career, the dominant feeling that comes to mind is uncertainty. On the outside, I looked composed, but inside, I felt small.

After graduating from the University of California, Berkeley, I didn't yet have a clear vision of where I was going. I tried on a few careers for size, but nothing seemed to fit. I struggled, not just professionally, but personally. At the time, I was caught in the grip of a severe eating disorder that quietly eroded my sense of self-worth. It was tied to a relentless perfectionism.

Eventually, I got myself into treatment, and that changed everything. For years, I thought I would become a physician, or perhaps a veterinarian, which felt like a natural fit for a horse-crazy girl. However, after being in therapy, I realized that what

I wanted to do was sit across from someone and help them navigate and understand their pain. I wanted to be a psychologist, and not just any kind of psychologist—I wanted to be a *psychoanalyst.*

I remember sitting in a clinical psychology class during my junior year of college, front row as always. The professor, Dr. Peter Newton—who would later become my dissertation chairperson—said, "Only psychiatrists and a very, very few psychologists ever become psychoanalysts."

Hearing him say that could have derailed my plans. After all, I wasn't aiming to become a psychiatrist. But I had a different reaction: Without hesitation, I thought, *No, I'm going to be one of those few.* I didn't tell anyone at the time—I just knew.

I've had similar moments of "knowing" throughout the years. For example, years earlier, when my trainer informed me that I would be riding in the children's hunter division for the next year, I nodded politely, but inside, I thought, *Absolutely not. I don't have the time. I'm not staying in this division. I have other places to go, like the Maclay Finals.* That was another moment of standing in what I knew was right for me. I wasn't dramatic or rebellious—just certain.

Something That Needs to Be Said

Those moments demonstrate how I handle it when someone challenges my competence. In hindsight, I realize that in my family, this was unique to me. That's not to say that my parents didn't struggle with deep fears of inadequacy. But they carried it differently: my dad through commanding power, my mom through unrelenting perfectionism.

That legacy of fear was passed down to me in subtle ways. As a young woman, I often wondered if I was smart enough, capable enough. I'd look around rooms and assume everyone else was sharper, quicker, more deserving, and when that fear crept in, I responded the only way I knew how: I worked harder.

The Protestant work ethic ran deep in our family, and to be fair, it got me through some tough seasons. But it also kept me locked in the loop of performance, always trying to prove my worth through effort, as if rest or ease were signs of weakness.

It's only now, with age and reflection, that I can say: *I am enough*. I have enough intelligence, enough intuition, enough presence. My questions are good. My insights are sound. I don't have to chase perfection anymore.

That grace didn't arrive overnight. It came slowly, through experience and therapy, through hearing others reflect back to me what I couldn't always see in myself.

Throughout my life, I have often experienced myself as the child in the story of *The Emperor's New Clothes*. I find myself in the role of the one who points out what others are too afraid to admit. I've never been the loudest voice in the room, but I've always been the one willing to speak the truth, even when it's uncomfortable. *Especially* when it's uncomfortable. When something seems glaringly wrong or ridiculously overcomplicated, I'll point it out. I'll say the thing that feels obvious, and people look around and say, "Oh yeah, good point." And I'm standing there wondering, *Was anybody going to mention that?*

This quality has followed me my whole life. I've been the one to ask the question no one else wants to ask, or to point out the elephant in the room that everyone else has politely ignored. That willingness to say, "Wait, this isn't right" has served me well, both in the therapy room and in the show ring. Horses, after all, don't care about your résumé. They respond to courage and calm. Maybe that's the lesson I needed all along: Show up, be present, trust your gut, knowing for sure that you are enough.

So let me say something to you that feels blatantly obvious to me, but no one seems to be saying it out loud:

> ***You are enough.* Right now, as you are. You don't have to earn it. You don't have to hustle your way into worthiness. You are already enough.**

We'll spend the rest of this book unpacking that. We'll explore how you can start showing up fully and authentically, expanding your life from a place of groundedness instead of guilt. But know this: You are not broken. You don't need to be fixed. And you certainly don't need to bend yourself into a pretzel to fit someone else's idea of "good enough." Remember, you're not "shrink-to-fit."

The Best Data We Have

I think many self-help and psychology books overcomplicate what's really quite obvious. I read them and think, *Come on, just say it already. Stop circling around the issue. Quit burying the lead.* That impatience is one of the reasons I'm writing this book in the first place. I got tired of waiting for someone else to say plainly, *You are enough just as you are. Go be fully you.* So here we are.

This goes all the way back to graduate school. I'd read psychological research studies and think, *You spent how much money to arrive at that conclusion?* Things that seemed so obvious would get packaged into complicated jargon, peer-reviewed and cited to death, as if they weren't plain as day to anyone actually paying attention.

I remember someone in my longtime workout group announcing there was "new research" showing that being around trees improves oxygen levels and boosts mood, and I just had to say, "Don't you think it's because being outside just feels good?"

She stopped for a second. "Oh," she said. "Good point."

Here's another obvious-to-me thing that I feel compelled to point out: We don't always need a study. Sometimes our own experience is the best data we have. You take a walk, you breathe, you feel better, not because a research paper told you so, but because your mind and body know. So yes, I'll be sharing ideas and tools in this book that are grounded in science *and* practice. Everything I tell you has grown out of my thirty-plus years of experience treating and coaching hundreds of women of all ages *and* the knowledge I've gained through my own personal experiences. But I'm also going to trust your common sense. I'm going to speak to you as the real person you are, not a subject in a clinical trial.

If at any point in this book you find yourself thinking, *Is it really that simple?*—yes, it just might be. Trust that. As I'll remind you often, you are enough.

KEY TAKEAWAYS

- You are enough, just as you are.
- When you start to question your worth, show up, be present, and trust your gut.
- You don't always need a study to prove something. Sometimes, your own experience is the only data you need.

PART II

THE INTERNAL MOUNTAINS WE CLIMB

THREE

MIXED MESSAGES AND THE WOUNDS THEY CAUSE

WHEN I TALK ABOUT DOUBT, FEAR, OR THE mixed messages women receive, I'm not just talking about what happens in childhood or in families. These messages come up in our adult lives as well—in the classroom, at work, in leadership, and in motherhood. For me, even after everything I'd overcome in childhood, I still carried an internal belief that I wasn't quite good enough. I had this rebelliousness inside me, a fire that wanted to spark up and push boundaries, but on the outside, I often came across as quiet and reserved. I wasn't sure the world really wanted to hear from me.

I eventually enrolled in the California School of Professional Psychology, where I earned my PhD in clinical psychology at age twenty-six. I might have gone to a more research-intensive school like UC Berkeley, but I chose not to apply. A professor at UC Berkeley later asked me, "Why didn't you apply here? You would've been a great fit." The truth is I didn't think they'd want me. A deep-seated doubt whispered, "They'll see you're not good enough."

I'd been hearing that same message from early on. My mother, who had been an English teacher before she became an attorney, would pore over all my school papers with a red pen and a critical eye. I submitted to it, but I dreaded it. It felt like every sentence was an autopsy, a dissection of all my flaws. Yet, at the same time, I owe her. Her scrutiny is part of why I know how to write today. I remember being at Wellesley College for a year and finally having to write papers on my own with no edits from Mom. I aced every single one, and when people told me I was a great writer, all I could think was, *Thanks, Mom. It was brutal, but it worked.*

But that nagging fear lingered. Even when I got positive feedback, I stayed closed off. Professors would say, "We wish you'd speak up more. You have good things to say." But I held back. I thought if I spoke up, I would reveal that I wasn't actually as smart as people thought. That somehow, I was faking it.

I see this same pattern in many women I work with today. They are accomplished, thoughtful, respected, but still unsure whether they truly deserve their success. They've internalized the idea that it's safer to shrink than to shine, or that humility means hiding their light to make others comfortable.

> **If that's a message you've downloaded too, then let me just say it here: *You don't have to underplay your brilliance to be likable or worthy*. You don't have to prove your worth again and again just to keep your seat at the table. If you've got the seat, use it. Don't wait for someone else's permission to take up space. You are not shrink-to-fit.**

Take the Compliment

One of the greatest mysteries I've observed in my clients, especially among high-achieving women, is their stunning ability to disregard clear, positive feedback. I'm not referring to ignoring compliments in passing. I mean refusing to believe hard, indisputable evidence that they're doing well and have something important to offer.

One of my clients is a smart, capable, forty-five-year-old woman with a high-stakes leadership position at a Fortune 200 company. She leads a big team, nails every deadline, and holds herself to the highest standards. She's the kind of person others admire for her competence and poise, yet she constantly walks the tightrope of self-doubt.

She's terrified of seeming too confident or too competent, so she downplays her contributions, constantly trying to be humble. Meanwhile, her senior leaders—her CEO and CFO—keep telling her the same thing: "We need more of your voice. Stop undercutting yourself." And still, she hesitates.

Ironically, she was recently promoted and given a raise. When I pointed this out to her, saying, "I think that's pretty clear evidence you're doing a great job," she shrugged it off.

She's also a dressage rider, which makes her self-doubt all the more fascinating to me. She bought a beautiful Thoroughbred—fancy, talented, the kind of horse you *show*—but she's hesitant to take him into the ring. Over and over, she would say to me, "He's not *a real* dressage horse. He's just a Thoroughbred." Her comment—that he's "just a Thoroughbred"—is a diminishment of both her horse and herself. She's hiding the fact that she bought a high-performance horse because at some level she wants to shine in the spotlight. She's afraid to admit her ambitions both to herself and to me. I had to ask her straight out, "So why did you buy a fancy dressage horse if you don't want to go in the ring? I mean, you're not planning to just hack him down the trail, are you?"

After a pause, she laughed and agreed that the contradiction was pretty glaring.

This pattern isn't something I see only in my adult clients. I see it in teenage riders too, like one young woman I coach who comes from a modest background. She has one horse of her own, but she's been earning her reputation through grit and results. Her trainer has been giving her catch rides—sale horses that need polish or confidence in the show ring—and she's delivering.

One day she was showing a fresh, unbalanced green horse. It was far from perfect, but she gave him a solid, confidence-building experience. When she came out of the ring, she started criticizing herself, focusing on what didn't go right. Her trainer, who was full of praise for her skill and effort, told her about another trainer who had been watching her and said, "I wish I had that kid riding my green horses."

High praise indeed, but this young rider couldn't take it in. She wouldn't let the praise land. When she retold the story to me, I had to stop her and say, "Wait a minute. Let's get this straight. You just rode a very green horse—a fire-breathing dragon of a green horse, no less—around a big show ring. You did your job. Not only did your trainer think you nailed it, but another trainer who didn't even know you wanted you riding for *her*. That's huge."

She agreed, but still, the doubt lingered.

This is something we as women have to confront directly, especially in the horse world. Riding gives us constant feedback: from the horse, from the judges, from our trainers, and from the people watching. Sometimes the feedback is fair and helpful; sometimes it's not.

But too often, especially as women, we don't absorb the good stuff. We cling to the criticisms and disregard the praise. We internalize the doubt and question the progress. It's no wonder we walk around feeling like we're not enough.

Even in my own life, I used to rattle off a mental list of all the reasons I wasn't as smart or accomplished as the people around me. I was afraid someone else might say it first—"You're not good enough; you don't belong here"—so I said it to myself before they could. It was a form of protection, but it was also self-sabotage.

Of course, feedback matters, but so does your ability to recognize when the world is giving you a green light. When someone hands you a compliment, a promotion, a catch ride, or a new opportunity, don't shrink. Don't diminish it. Don't brush it off with false humility.

Own it. That green dragon you just rode? You tamed it. That dressage horse you bought? He's waiting for you to step into the ring. That promotion you earned? It's real. Take it in. Trust it. Let it affirm what you already know deep down: You are capable. You are seen. You are enough.

The Courage to Begin

We don't come into this world fearless. We aren't born with confidence hardwired into our DNA. We learn it and build it. We grab it out of the moments when we feel least certain and most exposed. And honestly, a lot of the time, we just have to make a decision—to say, "I'm doing this" and keep moving forward until the rest of us catches up.

That's been my story, and it's probably yours too. I know because it's the story of so many women I work with. That creeping doubt, that whisper of "not-enoughness," shows up everywhere: in the boardroom, in the show ring, in our parenting, in our businesses, in our relationships.

Let me tell you something I've learned from working with hundreds of women: We often carry shame about being new to something. We forget that everyone—and I mean *everyone*—starts at the beginning. Nobody comes out of the womb with a PhD or a polished business plan or perfect equitation. We all begin somewhere, so why are we so ashamed of it?

I work with women all the time who are starting their businesses or launching something new, and they're paralyzed by this sense that they *should* already have it all figured out. They're afraid to ask questions, afraid to seek help, afraid to admit they're still learning, because somewhere along the way, they absorbed the lie that being *new* equals being *inadequate*.

The truth: We all have to start. And the only place to start is at the beginning.

I understand the feeling. When I was starting out, I felt ashamed of being at the beginning too. I thought I had to prove I was already good enough before I even started. That shame almost kept me from asking for what I needed. That's why I push back so hard on this now. It's not just wrong—it's damaging. It stunts our growth, and it isolates us from the support that's actually available if we just *ask*.

I remember a few years ago one of my clients—a young professional—was telling me about being at a major competition. She was feeling small, standing next to one of the big-name, world-class trainers. She imagined that he was judging her as she coached a rider of her own.

She was twenty-seven, talented, and doing a great job cultivating her own business. She was coaching her client at that show, but instead of embracing her own competence, she shrank from it. So I reminded her, "Own your stage, own your experience. There is no shame in being right where you are. There is no way that gentleman is expecting you to be him! Lean into who you are, and open yourself to learning from others who are farther down the road."

Yes, you'll have moments of doubt. Yes, you'll wonder if you're enough, and the answer is: *You are*. You are enough *right now*, not because you've mastered everything, but because you have the courage to begin.

There Is No Shame in Beginning

If you're standing next to someone who's more experienced than you, don't shrink—learn. That person might have a gem to offer, a small insight, a bit of perspective that opens something up in your own endeavor (whatever that endeavor is). If you let fear drive the moment, you'll miss it. That's where vulnerability comes in. Lean into the discomfort of not knowing everything. It doesn't mean you're weak. It means you're growing.

When I was younger, I didn't know how to do that. I kept a lot of my ambition quiet. I was afraid to say, "I want to be a psychoanalyst" out loud. It felt too bold, too exposed. I don't even know exactly why, but I imagined people would laugh or dismiss me: "Who do you think you are? You're not good enough for that."

So instead of reaching out or asking for help, I stayed quiet. I told myself a story that people wouldn't be there for me. But that story wasn't real. I created it. I built it out of fear, and it's one of the things I now work to dismantle in the riders and professionals I coach, especially the women.

Let's start right now. There is no shame in beginning.

You're not supposed to be as confident now as you will be in five or ten years. You're not supposed to know everything on day one. Whether you're stepping into the arena, opening your own business, or taking on a new role, the beginning is just that—the beginning. I was talking to a client about this very thing recently, and she said something that encapsulates it perfectly: *You get experience by getting experience.* Obvious, maybe, but it needs to be said!

As I told that young trainer, "Embrace where you are. You have a system that works with your clients. You're doing good work, and you still have things to learn. That's not shameful—it's honest."

That kind of reframing is what gives us permission to grow. It allows us to get out of the perfection trap and into a mindset where we can actually improve, connect, and thrive. When we stop expecting ourselves to have it all figured out, we start to show up in a whole new way. It lets us move forward without needing to pretend. It gives us permission to be bold, to ask questions, to admit when we don't know, and to receive help without shame.

Trust that you are enough, even if you're just starting. We all start at the beginning.

Small Acts, Big Lessons

Sometimes the moments that shape us most happen when we're new and shaky but still showing up.

A client told me a story that sums this up perfectly. When she was a kid, she rode Arabs, Anglo-Arabs, and the occasional Thoroughbred. Fancy warmbloods weren't part of her world. She was competing in a dressage test on her little Anglo-Arab mare, who, she told me, had a bolting issue, but they'd worked hard together and made it all the way to Second Level. For what it's worth, it was her first time ever showing at that level.

"I'll never forget that day," she told me. "I rode into the arena and saw the judge—it was none other than Hilda Gurney, former Olympian and dressage legend. The bell rang. I trotted in, halted at X, and then the bell rang *again*. I thought, *Wait, what?* I hadn't even started the test. I was completely confused.

"Then I heard her voice: 'Approach.' Still unsure what was happening, I walked my mare forward. She was spooking a little at C, nervous and edgy. Hilda stepped down from the judge's stand and came toward me. She said simply, 'Your girth is loose.' And then—this still blows me away—she reached down and tightened it for me. She didn't scold me or send me out. She just helped, then said, 'Trot around, compose yourself, and come back in to try again.'

"I was so intimidated already," she went on, "showing Second Level for the first time, judged by Hilda Gurney of all people. Nobody from my barn—including me—had checked the girth. Nobody said much at all besides 'Have fun' or 'Don't mess up.'

It could've been one of those moments that derails you completely, but instead, she treated me with kindness and gave me a chance to recover. I reentered the ring, rode my test, and we won the class with a 67 percent!"

That moment happened probably thirty years ago, but it has lived in her mind ever since. And when she told me the story, I was immediately struck by how powerful it was. What Hilda gave her that day was more than a tightened girth—she gave her a model for how experienced leaders can show up for someone new and not yet fully formed. She met my client where she was at the time and helped her stay in the game. That kind of small but meaningful support can make all the difference. It reminds us to be prepared, but also to notice when someone else needs help and extend grace.

The fact is, women need mentors. We need each other to step in, lend a hand, and lead—not compete. I don't see enough of it, and I know we can change that. I'm in a stage of life where I *should* be stepping into that mentor role. We all can. Hilda Gurney did. She had the experience and the authority, and she used it in the most generous way. And my client will never forget it.

It's those small, human acts of kindness that we carry forward. We remember them. We model them. We pass them on. A simple gesture from someone further down the path can help a younger, greener, more unsure person stand up straighter and believe they belong.

KEY TAKEAWAYS

- You don't have to diminish your brilliance to be worthy. And you don't have to wait for someone else's permission to take up space.
- Too often, women cling to criticisms and discard praise. When someone hands you a compliment, a promotion, or a new opportunity, take it in. Don't diminish it. Don't brush it off with false humility.
- Many of us carry shame about beginning. This isn't just wrong—it's damaging. It stunts our growth, and it isolates us from the support that's actually available if we just ask.
- If you're standing next to someone who's more experienced than you, don't shrink—learn. Lean into the discomfort of not knowing everything. It doesn't mean you're weak. It means you're growing.

FOUR

HOW WE SPEAK TO OURSELVES

HILDA GURNEY MADE A LASTING IMPRESSION ON my client because of her kindness and mentorship in a small moment of need. In contrast, I had an experience some years ago that left an impression not because it was uplifting, but because it showed me what *not* to do when someone is vulnerable and reaching out to learn.

It happened during a postgraduate supervision session I had signed up for just a few years into being a licensed psychologist. I was new to the field, eager to deepen my training by applying to the Psychoanalytic Institute. Becoming a Freudian analyst meant another five years of rigorous postgraduate work, but I was eager for it.

The Institute had invited a very well-known British analyst—an older woman who was famous in the field—to offer a few hours of case supervision to practicing psychologists. This was a rare opportunity. She wasn't staying long, and not all of her hours had been filled by graduate analysts, so I jumped at the chance to sit with her. I was nervous but excited, and deeply committed to learning.

I had just applied to the Psychoanalytic Institute for advanced training. I knew I had so much to learn, and I was excited but nervous to present one of my most challenging cases and gain feedback from someone with her level of experience. So I showed up early, dressed professionally, armed with notes and the hope that this brilliant woman might offer insights that would help me grow.

Finally, it was time for my session. I walked into her office, heart racing, and began to present.

About twenty minutes in, she interrupted me and said sharply, "This is *not* a psychoanalysis." And not in a gentle, constructive way, but as a complete dismissal of my work with the patient.

I froze. To a young clinician, that kind of statement was devastating. With that comment, she was dismissing the integrity of the whole treatment. At the time, I wasn't even in the Institute yet. I hadn't begun formal psychoanalytic training. Of course it wasn't a full psychoanalysis. However, instead of acknowledging that fact and helping me see the depth of what *could* be explored in the case, she shut me down. The message was clear: "Why are you even here?"

I was mortified. I'd paid a ridiculous amount of money for those hours, so I swallowed my pride and pushed through the rest of the session. I told myself, "Just finish what you came here to do." I got through it, but I walked away feeling small, unworthy, and as I thought more about it—angry.

That moment left a scar. She was a protégé of Melanie Klein, the early psychoanalyst I had studied in depth and written my dissertation about. Klein had been a student of Freud and had gone on to create an entire school of psychoanalytic thought. I deeply respected her work, and by extension, I respected this analyst. That made her dismissal cut even deeper. I never attended one of her sessions again.

That was more than thirty years ago, and I've never forgotten it.

What struck me then, and still does, is how easily she could have responded differently. She could have seen the intelligent, eager, aspiring young analyst across from her and lent her support. She could've said, "This doesn't quite sound like a formal psychoanalysis, but I see what you're working on." She could have encouraged what was there. She could have helped me see more deeply into the case, especially from a psychoanalytic perspective—perhaps bringing attention to transference, or to the subtle layers I hadn't yet learned to articulate.

Instead, she chose to judge rather than guide. It's a lesson I carry with me still, especially when I'm in a position to mentor someone newer, greener, and maybe unsure of themselves. That experience reminds me how much power we have in those moments. A few words can open a door or slam it shut. When someone is brave enough to ask, to present, to show up, they deserve respect and kindness—and a helping hand.

As leaders and mentors, we need to be the kind of people who meet others where they are, not where we think they should be. That's how we help them grow. That's how we build trust and change lives.

A teacher's job is to teach, help, and support. And yet, I can still vividly recall the sting of the moment when that didn't happen. Instead of encouragement, I received criticism so cutting that it stayed with me for decades.

It's tragic how often this happens—one woman undermining another, even though she knows exactly what that kind of treatment feels like. I've thought a lot about this. Why do some people who've experienced pain or exclusion themselves go on to inflict it on others? Is it unconscious? Habitual? A misplaced attempt to preserve hierarchy or control? I'm not sure. But I do know it's a pattern that must stop.

And that's why I share this story. If you've ever felt small, dismissed, or unseen in a moment when you were brave enough to step forward and learn, you're not alone. I've been there, but that experience taught me exactly the kind of mentor I want to be: the kind who sees effort, not just polish; the kind who welcomes growth, not perfection; the kind who helps others rise, instead of making them feel like they're inadequate.

No More "Justs"

Sadly, it's not just about how the people we look up to sometimes talk down to us. It's also about how we so frequently talk down to ourselves.

At a recent horse show, I witnessed one of those small but powerful moments that speak volumes about how women tend to minimize themselves.

I was walking my horse back from a hack, just cooling out and enjoying the moment. A woman passed by in a golf cart. I didn't know her, but I overheard someone approach and ask, "Are you a trainer?" She laughed a little and replied, "Oh, no, I'm just a rider." That word—*just*—hung in the air. I couldn't help myself. I called out to her and said, "You're not *just* a rider. You're a rider."

She was maybe in her thirties, young and earnest, and probably didn't even realize how much she was downplaying herself. But that's what so many of us do. We shrink ourselves with a single word. We use *just* as a disclaimer, a way to soften our presence, to avoid taking up too much space.

I've often noticed this pattern in barns and showgrounds. Riders, especially women, will say things like, "Oh, I'm just hacking today," or "I'm not going to ride with my trainer—I'm just going to ride by myself." As if that isn't enough. As if riding your horse—applying everything you've learned, staying mentally and physically present, working toward partnership and progress—isn't deeply valuable on its own. Somehow, we've picked up the idea that unless we're under the watchful eye of a trainer or actively preparing for a ribbon, what we're doing doesn't fully count.

But it does count. It all counts. Every ride, every quiet moment, every decision we make in partnership with our horses—and, more broadly, in our lives—matters.

You're not *just* anything. You're showing up. And that's enough.

We must be mindful of the ways we speak about ourselves and each other. These little verbal habits are more than just throwaway comments. They shape our self-image. They reinforce invisible hierarchies, and they either lift us up or shrink us down. So let's notice when we say "just," and let's choose to delete that word. You're not just a rider. You are a rider, and that's something to own with pride.

I know that sometimes this is easier said than done, so let me take this a step further: We have to help each other stop minimizing ourselves. Too often, it's automatic. A cultural habit so deeply ingrained that most of us don't even realize we're doing it. That's why speaking up, even in small moments, can make a difference.

The woman who said she was "just a rider" paused after I corrected her. Then she looked at me and said, "You're right. Thank you." And just like that, a little light flicked on. I was glad I said something. That small moment landed with her.

Supporting one another doesn't always require a formal mentor relationship or a grand gesture. Sometimes, it's just a sentence, a moment of seeing someone and offering them a new perspective. I believe the rider I spoke with will remember our interaction. And maybe next time someone at her barn says, "I'm just riding," she'll pass it forward. She'll say, "No, you're riding. Period."

That's how it works. We plant seeds, water them with compassion, and slowly, the culture begins to change.

"Go Ride Your Horse!"

When I was growing up in the hunter/jumper world, compliments were rare. Coaching was tough, often harsh, and far too often, personal. No one said, "You're doing X and Y really well; now let's work on Z." That sort of balanced, constructive feedback just wasn't part of the culture back then. Instead, the language was blunt, at times even cruel: "You're ruining that horse." Insults like that stick. I carry them in a vault somewhere with all the other things I wish had never been said to me.

It wasn't until my final year as a junior rider that I experienced something different. I had a big dream that year to ride in the Maclay Finals in Madison Square Garden. I was a bit late getting to that level, and in the middle of the season, right around July, I made a trainer switch. There was a lot behind that decision, but the heart of the story starts at Rancho Murieta. That's where I started working with Linda and Champ Hough of Sutton Place.

On the very first day, Linda—a National Show Hunter Hall of Fame rider and trainer—began schooling me for the Barbara

Worth Medal Finals. I was on my big hunter, a horse my previous trainer would have never allowed me to ride in a medal final. But Linda looked at him and said, "You need to ride the big horse in the final." She saw things differently. She didn't yell or berate. In an era when so many trainers screamed from the rail and weaponized their authority, Linda was calm, elegant, and direct.

I was nervous, of course. This was a big show. I jumped a few fences in the warm-up ring, and then Linda quietly called me over. She reached up, placed her hand gently on my leg, looked at me, and said, "You're a good rider. Go ride your horse." That's it. No lecture. No correction. Just belief. And something in me changed. I was a good rider? I don't think anyone had ever said that to me quite so plainly.

I rode that course with new confidence. There were three judges: I earned a 92 from one judge, a 90 from another, and a low score from the third. Only the last judge had noticed that my foot slipped out of the iron for one jump. But it didn't matter. I didn't win the class, but what I gained was worth so much more. Linda had set me free by acknowledging that I was enough and giving me permission to trust myself.

From then on, I started riding that same horse in the open four-foot classes, which had previously been reserved for professionals. And yes, I rode in the Maclay Finals at Madison Square Garden on that very horse. We didn't win, but we were on the standby list until the very end—twenty-fourth or twenty-fifth, right on the edge. It's one of the highlights of my riding life.

Linda's words—"Go ride your horse"—still echo. Even today, my current trainer uses that phrase when I start to get perfectionistic. If I'm overthinking, if nerves creep in, she looks at me and says it again: "Ride the horse." And I do, because I understand what that really means. It's not just about the mechanics of riding. It's about believing in yourself, showing up with confidence, and letting go of perfectionism.

That simple, human moment transformed me. It's the kind of mentorship we all need: calm, grounded, and generous. And it's exactly the kind of voice I hope this book can be for you, and you can be for the women around you.

Of course, you may not be a rider. I know not everyone reading these pages will be competing at a horse show, but that's just semantics. Everyone has moments when they need to show up more fully—whether it's in a boardroom, a classroom, or just in a tough conversation with someone they care about.

So come up with your own version of the phrase *Go ride your horse*—something short, potent, and personal that cuts through fear and self-doubt. Something you can say to yourself, or even ask others to say to you when you're struggling or spinning out. It might be "Speak your truth," or "Stand your ground," or "Just begin."

That kind of mantra is really about the freedom to be yourself and show up fully and authentically. Let's face it, we hobble ourselves. We trip over self-doubt, perfectionism, and criticism. We hesitate and overanalyze. But sometimes all it takes is the right phrase at the right moment to cut through the noise and say, *You're ready. Go do it.*

Go ride your horse did that for me, but it didn't apply to just riding. It also changed how I speak publicly. I used to get anxious before giving a presentation, even if I knew my material well, because I was afraid I might forget something or make a mistake. Eventually, I learned that the most powerful thing I can do is show up as *me*. To be present and connect with my audience. If I forget my train of thought, I'll find my way back. If something doesn't land, I can ask for feedback. I can adjust and adapt. I can ride the moment. It's enough to be me.

That's what *Go ride your horse* means to me now. Whether I'm walking into a show ring, standing on a stage, or sitting with a client, it's about being fully in the moment. Not worrying about Step Five when I'm on Step One. Not worrying about what the judge thinks or what I forgot to say. Just being right there, with clarity and intention.

This applies to every high-stakes moment. A job interview. A tough conversation. A moment of truth. Instead of shrinking, show up and ride through it. Trust yourself.

So, what's your phrase? What's your version of *Go ride your horse*? Find it and use it. Maybe even share it with someone else who needs a little nudge toward courage. Because one small phrase, repeated at the right time, can change everything.

The Danger of Self-Criticism

Self-criticism is one of the fastest ways to shut down your own voice. For example, if I'm giving a presentation and I suddenly start worrying that I'm not being articulate enough, I'll slip into a spiral of judgment. I'll hear that inner critic start to nitpick every word, and once that begins, my gears freeze up. I lose access to the part of myself that can communicate clearly and authentically. Creativity shuts down, and that's exactly the moment I have to intervene, stop the slide, and reclaim my voice.

Finding a mentor to help you learn to do that can help. Remember, a few well-timed words from a mentor can plant a seed that stays with you. As I said, for me, it all started with Linda Hough.

I actually saw Linda again at a show not long ago. She and her daughter Lauren—an Olympian and Pan American Games rider—were judging a big equitation class. I hadn't seen Linda in years, but when I spotted her, I walked up, gave her a hug, and said, "Can I tell you a story that's impacted my life?"

I reminded her of that moment in the warm-up ring when she said I was a good rider. I explained how those words gave me permission to trust myself. How I've carried them with me into so many parts of life. She was very touched, and I could see that it meant something to her too.

That's the beauty of it. Her words, spoken in truth, made an impact on my life that cannot be overstated. I'll never forget what she gave me, and I hope, through this book and through my work, that I have done the same for others.

It's important to seek out people in your life who see you—truly and authentically—and help mentor you. Often it's not just one person, but many people, who will do this for you in your life. We all need others to help us, because we can't fully do it for ourselves. But even if there's not someone in your life right now to speak grounding words to you, you can still start by *speaking them to yourself*. Be your own encouragement. Repeat your mantra when you need to hear it most. Speak confidence instead of criticism—and find ways to do the same for others in your life.

KEY TAKEAWAYS

- Be mindful of the ways you speak about yourself and others. Your verbal habits are more than just throwaway comments. They shape your self-image. They reinforce invisible hierarchies, and they either lift you up or quietly hold you down.

- Come up with a mantra—something short, potent, and personal that cuts through fear and self-doubt. Something you can say to yourself, or even ask others to say when you're struggling or spinning out. It might be "Speak your truth," or "Stand your ground," or "Let's begin."

FIVE

PERFECTIONISM: A DRIVER *AND* A DESTROYER

I'VE WORKED WITH MANY TYPES OF CLIENTS OVER the years, but there are three kinds of people—personas, really—that I most often support. To help ground them in your mind, I'll give each persona a backstory, because you may see yourself in one or more of them.

First, there's the accomplished, fifty-something executive. She's smart and mission-driven. On paper, she's thriving, but she hides her ambition. She's quietly afraid of her own success and unsure of what might happen if she truly owned her power.

Working with her means gently helping her step into her full brilliance by addressing the self-doubt and guilt that tell her ambition is something to conceal.

Then there's the thirty-something professional who is just starting to carve out her place in the industry. She's capable, talented, and deeply committed, but she's terrified of being "at the beginning." She doesn't want to look "foolish." She doesn't want to admit she doesn't know everything yet. There's this internal tension between her hunger to learn and her fear of looking like a beginner, and that fear can keep her stuck, shrinking herself, or hiding in the shadows of more experienced peers.

Finally, there's the teenage girl, an athlete still finding her voice both in and out of competition. Her story is about confidence, yes, but also about brutal perfectionism and brittleness. She is consumed by what she sees on social media. Deeply anxious, she is the opposite of resilient. To thrive, she must learn how to trust herself, to face pressure with grace, and to believe that her voice matters just as much as anyone else's, even in intimidating rooms.

What do all three of these personas have in common? In fact, what do most women have in common? Simply this: They struggle to show themselves the grace they need for where they are.

Wherever you are in life, whether you're aiming for the next level in your riding, stepping into leadership, or trying to live more fully, growth requires grace—for yourself and for the process. There's nothing wrong

with where you are. Keep going. This applies no matter who you are or where you are on your journey.

Take, for example, a woman I work with who's in her early thirties. She's a talented trainer in her own right, coaching riders who are working at an advanced level—some competing in Prix St. Georges, with others on their way there. She has clearly earned her place in the ring, yet she's often working alongside her own coach, who is coaching *his* riders at the same time. And in those moments, she feels small. It's not that she lacks skill or insight—it's that she's new to this stage of her career. Instead of owning that fact with grace, she sees her newness as something shameful.

She's a perfect example of someone who could benefit from a mentor voice—not someone to dictate or micromanage, but someone to gently affirm, "You're right where you need to be. Keep going."

The accomplished, fifty-something executive; the thirty-something professional; the teenage athlete—each of these people, at very different life stages, are navigating the same core question: *Do I belong here?* My answer, again and again, is: *Yes. You do.*

Joy in the Process

When I work with young riders, especially teenage girls, I often find myself addressing not only their mental and emotional readiness for performance, but also the immense pressure they carry on their shoulders. Sometimes, that pressure comes directly from their parents. It's something I've witnessed all too often, and it's heartbreaking every time.

Let me give you an example. Several years ago, I started working with a lovely family. The mother was intelligent and well-meaning, but she was unknowingly undermining her daughter's confidence. The father, while loving and supportive, did not attend most of the shows and seemed to be a shadowy presence at best.

Their daughter was about fifteen. She was a good kid with clear dedication to the sport, but her mother, who knew little about riding and hadn't made much effort to learn, constantly criticized her. I don't think she was trying to be cruel. In fact, I don't think she realized how critical she was. Still, the result was the same. The message this young woman was receiving, again and again, was that she was not enough. Not talented enough. Not serious enough. Not perfect enough. I knew the girl might not have fully internalized it yet, but the seeds were being planted.

I made it a priority to help the whole family break the cycle. However, this problem is bigger than one family, one barn, or one situation. It's even bigger than the sport of riding. It's everywhere in our culture. Too many high-anxiety parents are spoiling their child's experience because they are giving their kids the message that they aren't enough—not because they don't care, but because they care in the wrong ways.

What young athletes need to hear instead is, "You are enough." Yes, competition is hard. Yes, the journey can be frustrating. That's life. What matters is that they're showing up. They're trying. They're willing to fail and come back again. That's what builds character and resilience.

I see this dynamic in my practice all the time. Parents, often high-achieving themselves, come to me with a very specific agenda: They want me to help their child win. They want results. They want ribbons.

I, however, have a different agenda. I want to help their daughters and sons build confidence that doesn't crumble under pressure. I want to teach them how to find joy in the process, not just on the podium. And I want them to know that it's normal to fall short sometimes, that growth is messy, and mistakes are essential to mastery.

Honestly, some parents don't want to hear that. They want to buy their child's success like they buy their schooling or their shoes.

They want shortcuts, but there are no shortcuts to confidence. There's only practice, patience, and support.

Trainers and coaches tell me all the time how difficult it is to work with these kinds of parents. They come to me, exhausted and unsure how to help the kids under their care when the real pressure is coming from the sidelines. And I understand. It's hard when you see a young person full of potential shrink beneath the weight of someone else's expectations. It's hard when that potential is being sabotaged by a parent's unexamined anxiety.

So my message, to parents and professionals alike, is this: Support doesn't look like perfectionism. It doesn't sound like criticism. It doesn't focus solely on the outcome. Support means encouraging the process, honoring the effort, and reminding these kids constantly that they are enough, just as they are.

Blanket Pressure

So many young riders walk into my sessions weighed down by what I call "blanket pressure"—a heavy, suffocating layer of expectation they place on themselves to be perfect at all times. It's the kind of pressure that shuts down performance because it leaves no room for creativity, confidence, or even joy. The root of it often traces back to both internalized perfectionism and external criticism, especially from those well-meaning but misguided parents.

When a girl comes to me after a string of disappointing rounds, I don't start by analyzing her strategy or technique. I start by naming what's going on.

"Wow," I might say gently, "you're putting so much pressure on yourself right now."

By giving language to what they're experiencing, I often open the door for real change. We talk about how pressure is natural, even expected, in performance situations, but it doesn't have to be paralyzing. I teach them how to make pressure specific rather than generalized. To own it.

Instead of telling themselves, "I have to be perfect—I can't make a mistake," I guide them to focus on small, actionable goals.

By making their goals bite-sized and achievable, they often find their anxiety melting away. They perform better. They're more present. And yes, usually, the results improve too. But my real focus is helping them see themselves more clearly, and to find pride in effort and progress.

Even then, there's often resistance. After a great round, I might ask, "Are you proud of yourself?" And more often than not, the answer is "No, that would be cocky." It's such a common refrain among girls in their late teens. They're afraid that being proud of themselves will come off as arrogance. "I'd be too full of myself," they say, or "I don't want people assuming that I think I'm better than everyone else."

That's when I push back. I ask them, "If you set goals and you accomplish them, why wouldn't you be proud?" I challenge the idea that humility requires constant self-criticism. I want these young women to learn that to acknowledge and be proud of what they accomplish is courageous, not cocky. Registering our wins, both big and small, builds a foundation of internal confidence they can carry with them not just in the ring, but in every part of life.

In the end, I'm not just helping them become better athletes. I'm helping them become stronger, more confident, and more resilient young women, and that, in my book, is a championship worth winning.

There's a common belief that we can't fully acknowledge success because we might make a mistake tomorrow. I hear it all the time from my clients. They'll say things like, "Well, I did well today, but now there is so much pressure for tomorrow."

That's when I interrupt this thought pattern and direct them to owning their pressure: "What I need you to do is devote yourself to riding every step. Will your round be perfect? Absolutely not. No round is, and I don't know what perfect is anyhow. But you can be present and ride every step. Why is that important? Because your horse is going to suck back for a millisecond. Maybe he's going to get heavy on the forehand. Maybe he's going to drift right or left or spook at something. That's not failure. That's riding. What matters is how you respond—not that it happened, but what you did with it. I want you to focus on being effective, which means being present in every step. People focus so much of their energy on mistakes, and I want to draw your attention on what you aim to do and how."

Then I ask, "Is riding every step doable?" They always say yes, because it is. That's the standard: Show up, be present, ride the moment you're in. Not the one before, not the one after.

And then I remind them that just as there are challenges in every round, there are successes too. Some successes are invisible to everyone but you and maybe your trainer. Perhaps you came into a line and your instinct was to pull, because fear was tugging at you, but instead, you put your leg on, you stayed committed, and trusted yourself and your horse. No one in the stands saw that win, but you know it was there. And that counts. That's something to hover on.

Many women, however, hover on the negative, especially high-achieving, ambitious women. They'll walk me through every tiny thing that went wrong in their ride, their presentation, or their performance. Often, they've been thinking about those things for days, sometimes weeks. They let the negative eat away at them.

So, I say, "Let's look at what happened. Let's get curious and learn from it. What happened? What could you do differently next time?" But then, when we've talked through those things, I firmly say, "*Move on.*"

Rehearsing your perceived, or real, mistake over and over in your mind is the same thing as *practicing* it. Instead, I want them to rehearse the success. Replay the moments they were proud of. Celebrate the quiet wins. That's how we build confidence—not by avoiding mistakes, but by learning from them and choosing to hover on the growth.

Visualization is a powerful tool—I use it all the time with clients—but what most people don't understand is that *negative* visualization is also powerful visualization. When you mentally revisit a misstep, you're reinforcing that pattern psychologically and neurologically. You're deepening the groove.

So here is my invitation to you to break that cycle. Learn from the mistake, then *let it go*. Visualize how you want it to go next time, but more importantly, *savor* the parts that went well.

Savor the Successes

That word—savor—is essential. I don't want you to just *notice* the good moments. I want you to relive them. Anchor them in your memory and nervous system. That's the practice that builds confidence. That's the mental training that actually moves you forward. And yes, it feels good. That's not a bonus. That's the point.

You can physically ride your horse only so many times, but you can mentally ride as often as you want. You can visualize with intention and build a highlight reel of what success looks and feels like for you.

Savoring successes doesn't make you cocky. Being proud of something you worked for isn't arrogance. It's self-respect, and it's a solid strategy for improving performance.

Earlier, I mentioned the parents who were undermining their daughter's confidence. At a recent show, the mother was unable to praise her daughter's ride. When I said, "Wow, your daughter was great," she waved it off.

In this case, the mother was a high-powered litigator. She was in control of everything except her child. Her expectations were way off the mark—not to mention they were *her* expectations, rather than her child's. That's the problem. Many of these parents have spent their lives chasing perfection and performance. They project the same expectations and pressure onto their daughters. They think they're helping, but they're crushing their child's self-esteem.

This problem isn't limited to teenage girls. I see the exact same dynamic in grown women. You don't have to be fifteen to feel like you're never enough. The self-doubt, perfectionism, and relentless self-criticism doesn't magically go away with age. If anything, it calcifies.

That's why this work matters. That's why *Go ride your horse*—as a metaphor for being present, showing up fully, and letting go of perfection—applies to all of us. Whether you're fifteen, thirty-five, or fifty-five, it's about showing up fully and riding every step.

Recently, I spoke with a trainer who echoed what I've heard so many times before. She was frustrated, not *with* her student, but *for* her. As she explained, "I keep telling her she's doing better, that I'm proud of her progress, but it's like the praise just slides off. She doesn't hold on to it. She can tell me everything that went wrong, but she can't see what went right."

This dynamic is all too familiar. I see many athletes, especially young athletes who work hard and grow in measurable and meaningful ways, refuse to recognize their own growth. They deflect compliments and minimize their achievements. Even when they've worked for weeks on a technical challenge, when they finally get it, they brush off the win, already focused on the next perceived flaw.

So I recommended that the trainer pause and say, "Wait. I just told you I'm proud of you, and I meant it. Why are you dismissing that? Let's stay here for a moment." I encouraged her to lean in with curiosity and compassion, not correction. Often, there's something deeper going on. The rider is holding on to a story that tells them they're only as good as their last round, or their last ribbon, or their last perfect ride.

What we see in these girls is often a reflection of their mothers or the broader culture they're growing up in. We live in a perfectionistic society, especially when it comes to competition and performance. Many of these parents, especially mothers, are doing the same thing to themselves. They downplay their own accomplishments, rush past moments of pride, and fixate on what needs to be improved. Children mirror what we model—not what we say, but what we *do*.

There's a relentless emphasis on winning that compounds the problem. Social media and performance culture elevate first-place finishes while quietly devaluing the rest, but none of us win all the time. Even the best don't win most of the time.

The American Olympian Laura Kraut is one of my idols in the sport. She recently shared a beautiful social media post in which she reminded everyone that winning is rare. "We don't win," she wrote. "Not often. And that's okay. What matters are the small victories. The quiet breakthroughs. The personal milestones that don't come with a ribbon but mean everything to the rider who earned them."

That's where the joy is. And yet, in so many barns and households, we've lost sight of that. We're so focused on the outcome, the scoreboard, or the prize that we forget the process. We forget that progress isn't always visible in the arena. Sometimes, it's felt in a breath taken before a round or in the courage to try again after a fall. In the willingness to say, "That was hard. And I did it."

What I want riders, parents, and coaches to understand is that worth isn't tied to performance. Progress isn't always obvious, and accepting praise is not weakness. Let it in. Hold it. Sit with it. It's not arrogant to be proud. It's healing.

KEY TAKEAWAYS

- Growth requires grace—for yourself and for the process.
- Rehearsing your mistake over and over in your mind is the same thing as practicing it. Instead, rehearse the success. Replay the moments you were proud of. Celebrate both big and small wins. That's how you build confidence—not by avoiding mistakes, but by learning from them and choosing to hover on the growth.
- Your worth isn't tied to your performance. Progress isn't always obvious, and praise is not weakness. Let it in. Hold it. Sit with it. It's not arrogance to be proud. It's healing.

SIX

CHASING THE NEXT RUNG

LATELY, I'VE BEEN THINKING A LOT ABOUT HOW easy it is to lose a long-term perspective. We're raising a generation that's brilliant, ambitious, but deeply anxious. They want to get everything right, every time. They crave certainty, achievement, and measurable success, but what happens when they miss the mark?

A friend recently recommended a book called *The Anxious Generation* by Jonathan Haidt. Even before I read it, the title rang true. This is what I see every day, both in the barn and at home.

My younger daughter, Clara, is bright, driven, and a perfectionist—like so many of the young women I work with. Recently, she was upset with herself after missing a question on her organic chemistry test.

"I knew it," she told me. "I just knew it, and I didn't get it right." Her frustration was palpable.

"That's a bummer," I told her. "It stinks to miss something you knew. I get that. But keep going. You're doing an amazing job. This is hard stuff."

I didn't try to minimize it or turn it into a teachable moment. I simply acknowledged her disappointment, reminded her of her effort, and let it go. Soon after, she had moved on to the next class, the next goal, the next challenge.

That moment revealed something important about how high achievers process the world. For them, there's rarely time to sit with a mistake. There's barely space to acknowledge a win. They're in constant motion, chasing the next rung on the ladder. And when we, as parents or professionals, try to inject a little perspective or offer praise, it can feel like we're speaking a different language.

Shaping the Emotional Ecosystem

Whether they realize it or not, parents are shaping the emotional ecosystem their daughters live and perform in. Often it's the mothers who get blamed, but that's not my intention. I understand that many of them are carrying the same anxiety, the same perfectionism, the same hidden belief that being enough means doing everything perfectly, all the time.

The parents I see fall into one of two common types. Some are *uber-high achievers*—often executives or entrepreneurs, these are goal-driven people who are used to being in control and getting things right. They bring that same intensity to the barn, expecting progress on a timeline and performance without error. Their impatience is often unconscious. They are simply used to living at 100 miles per hour. They love their children fiercely, but they also tend to struggle with grace—for themselves and their kids—when things don't go according to plan.

Then there are the parents who are over-involved—whose identity is entangled with their child's performance. If the round goes well, they feel proud. If it doesn't, they feel crushed. Their over-involvement is born out of love, but it places enormous pressure on their children, especially their daughters, who internalize the unspoken message that their success holds emotional consequences for someone else.

Both of these types—the high achievers and the over-involved supporters—are trying their best, but they unintentionally reinforce the anxious mindset that makes performance less joyful and more stressful for the young women they're trying to support.

So, what do we do with this? We name it. We talk about it. We speak directly to the parents who are the quiet architects of their daughters' emotional landscapes. Our girls are always watching. They may not always hear what we *say*, but they're constantly absorbing what we *do*, including how we handle disappointment, how we treat ourselves, and how we define success.

If we want to raise resilient, grounded young women who know how to bounce back and find joy in the

journey, then we as parents have to model what that looks like. Not just at the showgrounds, but in everyday life.

The way we show up in our children's lives doesn't just influence their mindset in the ring—it shapes how they see themselves long after the ribbons are packed away.

When Parents Lose Perspective

At a recent competition, I watched a mother of a skilled junior rider hover near the ring. From her appearance, you might assume this woman had it all figured out. But the atmosphere around her was as heavy as a storm cloud. She was not loud or aggressive but quietly, relentlessly negative.

Her daughter would finish a round, and instead of cheering or even just smiling, the first words out of this mom's mouth were something like, "Ugh. Missed the lead change." There was always a sigh, a subtle shake of the head, as if disappointment had become her default setting.

What struck me most wasn't the criticism itself, but rather how normal and casual it seemed to her. I don't think she was trying to be cruel. In fact, she probably thought she was being helpful, observant, maybe even motivating, but what she was actually doing was diminishing her child's effort with every word.

This girl is a good rider. She's hardworking and passionate, in love with her horse and determined to improve, but the energy from her mother made it feel like nothing was ever enough.

There are many parents like this in riding and other competitive sports. Parents who judge their child's athleticism as if it's a reflection of their own value. These are parents who start conversations with "Why didn't she win?" or "There must be something wrong with her."

What's missing is perspective.

Why do we put our kids in sports in the first place? We do it because sports, especially those as complex and humbling as competitive riding, teach life. They build discipline, grit, and resilience. They teach our kids how to win and lose graciously, how to fall off and get back on. Sports help them learn who they are under pressure, how to navigate setbacks, and how to trust themselves and their partners.

When you're twelve and competing in a horse show, the biggest win isn't the ribbon—it's finishing your round, facing the nerves, remembering your course, and trying again the next day. If you miss a lead change, that's not failure. That's just the sport.

Yes, riding is hard. We all know this. That's part of what makes it so worthwhile.

What I want more parents to value is not winning, but rather deep engagement. I want this for my own children also. I yearn for them to pursue a life of purpose and to find joy in the process, not just in the results. I want them to be in the arena, literally and metaphorically, giving it their all, and learning who they are along the way.

My middle child, Adele, started college during the heart of the pandemic. Her senior year of high school and freshman year of college were overshadowed by the many challenges of COVID-19. In-person classes, sports, and ceremonies of all kinds were canceled, unique experiences lost.

But here's the thing: School didn't always come easily to her. Her success at an elite university wasn't just an academic victory—it was a triumph of character. She worked tirelessly to achieve her goals, recently graduating from the University of Notre Dame. She is now on her way to becoming a psychologist.

Our children's paths aren't supposed to be smooth. They're supposed to be meaningful.

> **When we, as parents, focus only on perfection, we miss the beauty of what's unfolding right in front of us. We miss the growth, the passion, the effort. We miss our kids becoming *themselves*.**

So if you're a parent reading this, I invite you to step back and reframe. Watch your daughter ride, not as a judge, but as a witness to her bravery. Celebrate the stumbles and the recovery, not just the ribbons. Ask yourself, "Am I helping her grow, or just pressuring her to perform?" Trust me, if she's anything like the teenagers I work with, she already has plenty of internal pressure to perform. She needs your support and admiration, not critique or pressure.

Remember, the way we show up—at the shows, at home, in everyday moments—is the environment our daughters will carry into their adult lives. Let's make it one of encouragement, not critique, and of self-respect, not shame.

"I Can Figure Stuff Out"

One of my proudest moments as a mom came at the end of my daughter's freshman year of college, in the middle of a completely ordinary conversation. She looked at me and said, "Mom, I really feel like now I can figure stuff out."

That was it. Not "I'm perfect," or "I crushed it," or "Everyone thinks I'm amazing." It was so much more than that. *I can figure stuff out.*

I remember thinking, *Touchdown! How powerful is that feeling!* At that moment, I knew she'd be fine in life. She didn't feel the need to be flawless. She knew how to reach out for support, how to ask for help, how to lean on her internal and external resources. My daughter had developed what every mother ultimately hopes to cultivate in her child: secure, grounded confidence in her own capacity.

That's real power—not a flawless record, but the belief that you can navigate through challenges. That's what we want for our kids. That's what we want for ourselves. Sadly, far too often, I see loving, well-meaning parents diminishing that exact strength in their children. Sometimes it's subtle: A brief frown after a round in the ring. A passive comment like, "Well, you always miss that lead change." Other times it's more overt: "What's wrong with you?" or "You'll never make it at this rate."

That voice, even when it's quiet, cuts deep because it replaces "*I can figure it out*" with "*There's something wrong with me.*"

Many women who are anxious have internalized a belief that discomfort is dangerous and mistakes mean failure. They pass that fear on, sometimes with the best intentions, but the result is the same: children who feel they have to be perfect and can't see their own strength.

One of my longtime clients—a mother of two boys—is an example. She carries a constant sense of anxiety about things going wrong. When life gets tough, her first instinct is panic. Her sons have picked up on that energy, and it has become part of their internal narrative: *When something hard happens, we don't have what it takes.*

I've worked with her to reframe that response. We've talked a lot about the importance of sending a different message: *We may not know the answer now, but we can figure it out.*

That's the mindset I want to promote. Riding, like life, isn't about winning all the time. It's about showing up every day. It's about making a mistake, learning from it, and coming back tomorrow a little stronger. It's about falling, brushing yourself off, and getting back in the saddle. And it's about knowing—not hoping, not pretending, but *knowing*—that you have what it takes to figure it out.

That doesn't mean you never ask for help. In fact, it means the opposite. When you believe you can figure things out, you know how to find your resources. You know how to call a trainer, ask a vet, reach out to a friend, or maybe even reread a chapter in this book.

Whether you're a teenager struggling with pressure, a parent trying to support your child effectively, a trainer balancing your own perfectionism, or a high-achieving executive learning to embrace vulnerability—the real goal is developing the freedom and confidence to take on a challenge. It's having the courage to be curious instead of fearful, and the strength to say, even when you're shaking in your boots, "I've got this. I'll figure it out."

That's the foundation of resilience, and that's what we're building here.

Not Knowing Everything

One of my clients, a young professional, came to me because she was consumed with doubt. While she was doing all the right things—building her client base, holding clinics, coaching at shows—beneath the surface, she constantly doubted herself. She was a smart, capable woman in her early thirties who was clearly wrestling with something deeper than technique.

She didn't doubt her skills per se, but she was in the early stages of her journey and didn't yet have all the answers. Unfortunately, our culture doesn't celebrate that space.

That mindset is suffocating. It shuts down our ability to learn, adapt, and grow. It creates rigidity. It traps us in performance mode, always trying to *seem* like we know instead of genuinely *learning*.

As I mentioned earlier, this is a pattern I see everywhere. When we're ashamed of not knowing, and when we see learning as weakness, we miss out on our greatest opportunities for growth. We begin to armor up, trying to "fake it" instead of embracing the truth of where we are.

If you've experienced this firsthand, you might wonder how to start to break out of that trap. The answer: Ask yourself, *What's so terrible about not knowing? Where did I learn that I'm not allowed to be a beginner?*

Remember, there is no shame in being at the beginning. Everyone begins somewhere. The point is to start and then keep going.

We all start at the beginning.

As I mentioned earlier, the only way to get experience is to get experience. As an addendum to that, the only way to gain *confidence* is to gain experience. You master something by doing it, again and again and again.

There are no shortcuts to mastery.

When I discuss these concepts in a client meeting, their reaction is usually to be surprised. It's like no one's ever given them permission to *not know*. No one's ever said, "You're five years in. You're allowed to be learning."

Here's what I want every ambitious, self-critical, overwhelmed woman to hear:

Being at the beginning doesn't make you less valuable. It makes you brave. It means you're investing in mastery,

and mastery takes time. The only mistake you can make at an early stage is trying to skip it.

So whether you're a trainer, a parent, a psychologist, or someone in the middle of a major identity shift, let my words remind you: You don't have to know everything. You have to stay curious. Most importantly, you must stop judging yourself for not being ten years ahead of where you are. The people you admire were at this early stage once as well.

Everyone begins.

One of the most powerful breakthroughs I see in the women I work with is when they finally acknowledge the quiet shame they carry about not being more advanced. It often starts with a subtle comment: "I feel like I should know more by now." *Should*. "Should" is almost always a red flag.

When I hear it, I pause. I say, "What's the shame in not knowing *yet*?"

Many haven't even realized that this internal pressure exists. They've never noticed that they've been holding themselves to an invisible standard of mastery long before it's even reasonable to expect it. They think they're supposed to know it all by year one, or even month six.

So I ask, "In a year, do you think you'll feel more confident than you do now?"

They nod. "Yes."

"And in five years?"

"Of course."

"And in ten?"

"Definitely."

Then I gently say, "Exactly. That's how it works."

Experience takes time. Growth takes time. Mastery takes time. These truths sound obvious, but in a culture addicted to instant success and crafted perfection, we need to be reminded.

Imagine a child in first grade, just beginning to read. Is there shame in not knowing how to read on day one? Of course not. We honor that phase. We know it's part of the process. Why should it be any different for professionals?

I often use myself as an example. When I was training to become a psychologist, I had to do my first intake. I had to ask my first questions. I wasn't confident because I had no experience yet. But I started. I wasn't perfect, but I began. And there was no shame in that.

We forget how many things in life we've already started from scratch. Our first yoga class. Our first paper in third grade. Our first ride. No one expects you to walk into the arena or the therapy office with ten years of wisdom and seasoning under your belt. That comes *with time*. There is no substitute for experience.

Once you embrace where you are—whether you're a third-year trainer or a second-year psychologist—you get to work from there, instead of pretending you're somewhere else. That doesn't mean you're settling. It means you're honoring your place on the journey and trusting that confidence will come, not because you force it, but because you earn it. It won't come all at once, but ride by ride, client by client, lesson by lesson, and day by day.

KEY TAKEAWAYS

- If we want to raise resilient, grounded young women who know how to bounce back and find joy in the journey, then we as parents have to model what that looks like.
- When we as parents focus only on perfection, we miss the beauty of what's unfolding right in front of us. We miss the growth, the passion, the effort. We miss our kids becoming themselves. So if you're a parent, I invite you to step back and reframe. Ask yourself, "Am I helping my child grow, or just pressuring them to perform?"
- The way we show up is the environment our kids will carry into their adult lives. Let's make it one of encouragement, not critique, and of self-respect, not shame.
- Whether you're a teenager struggling with pressure, a parent trying to support your child effectively, a trainer balancing your own perfectionism, or a high-achieving executive learning to embrace vulnerability—the real goal

is developing the freedom and confidence to take on a challenge. It's having the courage to be curious instead of fearful, and the strength to say, even when you're shaking in your boots, "I've got this. I can figure it out."

SEVEN

BUILDING CREATIVE CONFIDENCE

JUST THIS WEEK, ONE OF MY CLIENTS, A WOMAN in her third year of being a professional, came to me flustered and overwhelmed. She was fretting about what medications and supplements to give her horses at an upcoming show.

"So-and-so uses this and this," she said, "but then another trainer does it completely differently. I just don't know what to do."

Her anxiety wasn't really about magnesium or electrolytes. It was about uncertainty, and her belief that there must be one perfect answer out there that she hadn't found yet.

This, I told her, is the trap: the belief that there's a single "right" way to do everything. That perfection exists if you can just crack the code.

I interrupted her frantic list of comparisons and said, "You already have a system. You've made choices. You've developed routines that work for you now. What you decide to do today might evolve in three months. You may drop a supplement or add something else. That's not failure. That's growth."

There is no single formula or flawless blueprint. Ask five respected trainers how they prepare horses for a show, and you'll get five different answers. Chasing someone else's perfection only distracts you from your own emerging wisdom.

To that anxious trainer, I offered a three-part challenge: 1) Acknowledge what you *do* know. 2) Recognize your progress. 3) And resist the pull of perfectionism that whispers, *You're still not enough*, because that voice crushes creativity. And creativity is essential in this work.

If you struggle with the same thought—the idea that there's one perfect system, and it's not yours—let me invite you to do the same.

In the world of horses (and business, parenting, coaching, and a million other things), your greatest asset is your willingness to think creatively and evolve. "What does this horse need today? What will best serve this rider at this moment?" When you're stuck looking outward, trying to replicate someone else's "perfect" system, you're not really present or using your intuition. You're not free to think creatively because you're stuck in fear.

Creativity requires risk. That means the risk of being wrong. The risk of starting over. The risk of wasting a paragraph or a ride or a week just to realize you're going in the wrong direction. That's not failure. That's the process.

We have to be willing to play, experiment, and iterate, which means we have to be okay with scrapping something that doesn't work. Accept that your value doesn't crumble if you make a mistake. If we become so fragile that we can't tolerate being wrong, we lose the very power we're trying to build.

This applies in the barn. It applies in life. It applies to me and to all of my clients. And it absolutely applies to you. You don't have to know everything. You just have to stay curious and brave enough to keep creating.

The Freedom to Grow

I want to help you stay connected to your instincts and your creativity, not just in the show ring, and not just when you're coaching or riding, but in all things. When we succumb to perfectionism, comparison, or shame, we narrow our perspective; we shrink ourselves and we cut ourselves off from possibility and growth. We lose our sense of play, and when that happens, we lose the very environment that allows learning to flourish.

If you approach challenges with a playful mindset, mistakes don't mean failure. They become part of the process. You can say, "Okay, that didn't work. Let's try something else." You stay open and curious, which allows you to move forward. However, when the atmosphere is rigid, critical, and fearful, your learning shuts down, and creativity goes silent.

Did you know that scientists regard a "failed" experiment as worthwhile data? Adopt that mindset. Learn from your mistakes, and move on!

There's a young rider I'm working with—seventeen years old—whom I absolutely adore. She's kind, earnest, and incredibly hardworking. She dreams of becoming a professional one day, and her commitment is rock-solid.

Currently, she is training in a prestigious program, but the environment is what you might call "old school." The head trainer is deeply experienced and highly respected, but her methods are harsh. Her motto could be: "*This is how it's done. Do it this way. Don't question. Don't stray.*" There's no room for curiosity or independent thinking, and certainly no room for play.

The head trainer is not a consistent presence. She floats in and out. She's the figurehead, the authority. When she arrives, the tone in the barn shifts instantly. The air gets heavier, and you can feel the pressure rise.

Now, this young rider is doing her best. She wants to impress. She wants to do everything *right* so badly that it's impossible for her to perform like she knows how. She's losing her voice and her light. Under the pressure, she is becoming afraid to try things. Afraid to fail.

I think it's heartbreaking when our desire to do well turns into fear of getting it wrong. This is exactly why creativity matters, and why fostering independent thinking is so important, especially for young women.

When someone is allowed to play, they learn faster. They take more ownership of their journey because they're not parroting someone else's rules. Instead, they're developing judgment, instinct, and resilience. They are learning how to *figure it out*, not just how to follow.

Play is not the opposite of professionalism. It is the foundation of mastery. When we allow space for creativity, especially in the formative years of training, we unlock the joy and growth that perfectionism can never deliver.

The Power of Belief and the Cost of Control

Whenever the head trainer is away, my young client works with an assistant trainer. The difference is night and day. The assistant trainer trusts my client. He believes in her skill, but more than that, he believes in her ability to figure things out. There's a sense of play, of give and take. He is present, observant, and encouraging. He's teaching her to think, not just to follow.

She once told me, "When I ride with him, I can jump a course and if it doesn't feel quite right, I just do it again. We talk about it. It's easy. It's fun. I ride so much better with him."

But as soon as the head trainer returns, all her confidence evaporates. She shrinks.

"I can't ride," she told me, after one difficult lesson. It's the same kid with the same talent on the same horse, yet she was completely undone.

What changed? The head trainer doesn't allow her to think for herself. This young rider desperately wants the head trainer's approval. She wants to be seen and praised, but the trainer leads with criticism and control instead of connection and trust.

Here's a perfect example. They were doing the "circle of death" exercise—four poles evenly spaced on a circle, with four strides between each. It's a notoriously difficult drill. If you miss your track even slightly, the whole pattern collapses. That's the challenge, and the brilliance, of the exercise.

So she's riding the circle with the head trainer. She makes the strides, but it's a bit rigid, a bit mechanical. The trainer yells across the ring, "Make it smoother!" And then she has my client do it again. And again. And again. Twenty times.

Each repetition chips away at her sense of self. She's no longer learning. Now, she's just trying to survive the ride. She abandons her own thinking entirely because all she can focus on is earning the trainer's approval. Ultimately, the whole thing collapses.

Afterward, she tells me, "I think I should just toss that trainer out of my head and ride like I do with the assistant trainer."

You know what? She was exactly right.

If the head trainer had said, "That was a solid try. You got the strides. Now just smooth it out a little—go again, I know you've got this," the outcome would've been completely different.

That's not coddling. That's coaching. That's the head trainer saying:

- I see your effort.
- I trust your ability.
- I know you can improve.

That kind of support unlocks something important. The student stays open and present, willing to try again out of confidence.

Instead, the message she absorbed was: *You're not good enough. You're doing it wrong. You don't belong.* Consequently, she walked out of that ring believing she couldn't ride, which, of course, is completely untrue.

What happened at that lesson wasn't about messing up the circle of death. It was about the tone, the energy, and the absence of belief. When trainers lead with curiosity and trust, riders grow stronger and braver. When they lead with control, rigidity, and judgment, even the most promising students begin to wither.

This is true in riding, and it's true in life. The energy behind the correction matters as much as the correction itself. If we want to develop resilient riders and resilient human beings—or become resilient ourselves—we have to create space for thinking, experimenting, and recovering from mistakes without shame. And if nobody is willing to do that for us, we have to find a way to do it for ourselves.

Don't Abandon Yourself

After my client explained the situation to me, I remarked, "You abandoned yourself."

She looked at me, startled, and then nodded slowly. "I did," she admitted. That was the heart of it.

Yes, the head trainer was in the ring, commanding and critical as ever, but the real issue wasn't the trainer's tone or the difficulty of the exercise. The issue was that the young rider had abandoned her own inner compass. She handed over all her power, creativity, decision-making, and trust in herself to someone else. In doing so, she lost her confidence and her sense of self.

Young athletes, in particular, want so badly to please, to be good, to get it right, that they'll shrink themselves in the presence of someone authoritative or intimidating. But this is exactly the moment when they need to stay grounded and connected to who they are. *Especially* when authority figures show up.

Sadly, that head trainer doesn't see my client for who she really is, and if a trainer can't see their student, they can't truly believe in them. They can't offer meaningful support because their validation is conditional and transactional.

The assistant trainer, on the other hand, sees her completely. He sees her dedication, her skill, her love for the horses, her willingness to work hard and grow. His belief in her is rooted in observation and relationship, and it allows my client to stay connected, to experiment, and to learn from mistakes without shame. That kind of belief doesn't evaporate with a missed distance or a flubbed lead change. It holds steady.

It's the same belief I offer my own kids. When my daughter struggled with organic chemistry, I didn't panic or jump in to fix it. I simply said, "You're a great student. You work hard. You'll figure it out." Because I knew she would. The underlying message: *I believe in you, I'm here if you need me, and mistakes don't undo your value.* When a young person internalizes that message—*I can figure it out*—they stop abandoning themselves. They learn to stay steady no matter who walks into the ring.

The Inner Critic

Whether it's a teenage rider trying to prove herself in the arena or a fifty-something executive in a corner office, the internal battle is often the same. It's the inner critic—that relentless voice of doubt, shame, and perfectionism that tells you you're not doing enough, not getting it right, not measuring up.

The same dynamic I see in young professionals shows up in older, accomplished women—some of them riders, some of them not. Just the other day, I was working with a client in her late forties who is wildly successful by any external measure. She holds a senior leadership position at a major corporation and consistently receives great performance reviews. Even so, she constantly questions her abilities.

"I don't know if I'm doing a good job," she says. "I just feel like I'm going to disappoint someone."

This is a woman who leads major initiatives. She commands respect, but she's haunted by a persistent fear that she'll let people down.

I explored this feeling with her. "What if you *did* make a mistake?" I asked her. "What if someone *was* disappointed?"

Her mind began to race, conjuring worst-case scenarios and imagining consequences that hadn't happened. It became clear that she has a deep-seated fear that she would be exposed as not good enough. That same fear follows her into the saddle. She's a dedicated hunter/jumper rider, and as she prepared for an upcoming show, she started to panic.

"What if I fall off?" she asked.

Her horse is solid. He's not spooky, and she hasn't fallen off in ages. She's experienced and focused, so the data just didn't match the fear. I pressed her: "Is it really about falling off? Or is it about something else?"

She paused, and then the truth surfaced. She admitted that her real fear was disappointing others and failing to meet their expectations. The riding arena had become another stage where the fear of not being enough played out.

And it's not just her. Another client—a C-level executive at a large company—struggles with a similar pattern. She's competent and respected in the boardroom, but in the barn, she becomes a self-doubting beginner. She holds herself to impossible standards and is terrified her trainers won't like her. She wants to be the best student, the best rider, the best everything, immediately.

Both women are shrinking themselves under the pressure of their relentless inner critics. Despite all their achievements, they don't *see* themselves clearly. Even if others believe in them, they can't internalize that belief because their own inner critic is louder. They suffer from the same inability to embrace imperfection. It's a common fear, but it blocks curiosity and sabotages growth—not just in the arena, but in every corner of life.

What I want for these women—for all of us—is not just to silence the inner critic, but to *replace her* with a more compassionate voice that says, "I see you. I believe in you. You're allowed to learn."

Remember, confidence isn't the absence of fear or failure. It's the presence of self-trust, and that's what gives us the courage to show up, both in the ring and beyond.

KEY TAKEAWAYS

- There's a trap many women face: the belief that there's a single "right" way to do everything. But there is no single formula or flawless blueprint.

- Chasing someone else's perfection only distracts you from your own emerging wisdom. So, let me invite you to reframe. Acknowledge what you do know. Recognize your progress. And resist the pull of perfectionism that whispers, "You're still not enough," because that voice crushes creativity.

- Play is not the opposite of professionalism. It is the foundation for developing mastery. When we allow space for creativity, especially in the formative years of training, we unlock the joy and growth that perfectionism can never deliver.

- If we want to become resilient—or develop resilient kids—we have to create space for thinking, experimenting, and recovering from mistakes without shame.

EIGHT

EMBRACING COMPETENCE

WHY IS IT THAT SO MANY HIGH-ACHIEVING women, whether they're in the saddle or sitting at the head of a conference table, are so reluctant to embrace their own competence? They don't enjoy it, and worse, they're continually haunted by the fear that one misstep could undo it all.

One of the clients I mentioned in the last chapter is a perfect example of this tension. She's deeply respected at work, and her team values her input. By all measurable data, she's doing a fantastic job, and yet, she doubts herself every day.

She's afraid of disappointing someone. She's afraid of saying the wrong thing in a meeting. She creates disaster scenarios in her head—scenes where she makes a major error, gets fired, loses all credibility. These fears aren't grounded in reality, but they still hold tremendous power over her. When we look at the facts, the fears don't add up. I'll say to her, "The data just doesn't support that fear." And she'll laugh because she knows it's true, but still, it lingers.

The root of this conflict isn't incompetence. These women are tough as nails in the eyes of the world, but internally, they are afraid to take risks, afraid to speak freely, afraid to fully show up as themselves.

I asked this client recently, "Why can't you enjoy how good you are at what you do? Why can't you trust that your experience, wisdom, and skill will carry you? Why do you brace yourself, even in rooms where you are respected and wanted?"

The truth is, she's limiting—shrinking—herself. Her company doesn't want a robotic version of her. They want *her*. They want her creativity, her voice, her leadership, but she's so worried about being liked or getting it right that she doesn't contribute as robustly as she could. She doesn't take the risks that would elevate both her career and the organization.

Interestingly, in the show ring, the work she and I are doing together is allowing her to change. Where she once was rigid and self-critical, she's now more playful, testing things, making adjustments, riding with intuition instead of a demand for technical perfection. That evolution has opened up a whole new dimension of enjoyment and progress in her riding. The goal now is to bring that same playfulness into her work life.

Creativity doesn't thrive under blanket perfectionistic pressure. Appropriately applied pressure—the kind that lifts up our ability to perform—is helpful and necessary for growth. But creativity needs space and breathing room. Most of all, it needs *permission* to get it wrong, to try it again, to be human and imperfect.

For so many women, the drive to be perfect and the need to be liked tend to combine in destructive ways. It's the voice that says, "You have to work twice as hard to be taken seriously," fused with the fear of letting anyone down. It leaves women feeling exhausted and isolated. What if we turned that narrative on its head?

What if competence wasn't a mask we had to constantly maintain, but a well we could draw from? What if we didn't need a blue ribbon or a perfect review to validate growth? What if we believed, deeply and fully, that our mistakes didn't disqualify us but made us *more* competent?

The Rider Who Couldn't Hold the Joy

There's another high-performing, highly competent rider I work with, a woman in her fifties, who seems from the outside to have it all together. She is a partner at a successful law firm, and she's a decorated rider with big wins under her belt. She has proven herself time and time again both in her professional life and the ring, yet she still can't seem to give herself permission to enjoy any of it.

She's relentlessly hard on herself. Even when she succeeds, she barely pauses before launching into her next set of expectations. When things don't go according to plan, the criticism she directs at others often masks the fact that she's turning that judgment inward, lacerating herself with accusations of not being good enough.

There's a brittleness to her that comes not from weakness but from unrelenting standards. She struggles to recover emotionally from setbacks, even small ones. There's little elasticity in her self-regard and no self-compassion to absorb the impact of imperfection.

Not long ago, she made a request. "Could you text me in the morning," she said, "and remind me that I can do it—and that this is supposed to be fun?"

At first, I was puzzled. This is a woman who is a powerful attorney. She's been wildly successful, both professionally and athletically, yet here she was, asking for a reminder that she's good and that she can enjoy herself. That she's allowed to show up for her horses with lightness, confidence in herself, and trust.

In my analytic days, I would have asked about her request, trying to unpack the need and question the dependency. Now, I simply said yes, and from then on, whenever she asked, I would send her a message that echoed the one my own trainer once gave me: "*Go ride your horse.*"

That's right: There's that phrase again. *Go ride your horse.* No need to overthink. No need to carry the weight of a lifetime of pressure into the saddle. Just show up, do your thing, and remember why you love this.

What strikes me, though, is *why* she needs that reminder. Why is it so hard to hold onto joy? Why must she outsource permission to feel good about something she's worked so hard to earn?

For her, my message wasn't just about horses. It was about helping her to remember her worthiness so she could loosen the grip of perfectionism and remind herself that she's already enough. She doesn't have to be flawless to be allowed to enjoy her horses. She doesn't need to earn joy through pain.

What she was really asking for was perspective from someone else—because it's hard to do it for yourself if you don't have other people helping. I was willing to give that perspective, because what I really want is for her, and every woman like her, to *hold on to* the joy and the solid confidence in herself. To feel it in her bones. To know, without needing external validation, that it's okay to trust herself and to fully live.

Sometimes, what we need most isn't more skill, more accolades, or even more experience. We need permission. So many of my clients aren't really asking for more instruction. They're asking (sometimes silently, sometimes directly) for permission. Permission to enjoy what they're good at without guilt or apology—permission not to shrink.

I've had similar conversations with many riders, and I often find myself saying something like, "You're a good rider. You clearly know what you're doing. What if you leaned into that? What if you allowed yourself to enjoy your competence?"

Most of them struggle with this instruction. Enjoying your competence doesn't mean you expect things to go perfectly. It means you acknowledge your competence and how far you've come. You stop obsessing over the one thing you think you lack and start leaning into all that you've built.

For me, one of the unexpected joys of being in this phase of life is that I've lived enough, learned enough, fallen enough, and stood back up enough to know I'm good at what I do. I know how to feel my way through tough conversations because I've done it for many years. I can talk to anyone, find the thread, and follow it. I make mistakes, of course, but they no longer rattle me or threaten my self-worth. They're part of the process.

> This is the kind of freedom I want for every woman I work with. It's the kind of freedom I want for *you*. It comes when you stop waiting for someone else to tell you you're allowed, and you start giving yourself permission to show up as the skilled, growing, powerful woman you already are. *To become unshrinkable.*

The Power of Raising Your Hand

For much of my earlier career, I sat in seminars or meetings and felt this deep, anxious resistance to raising my hand. Even if I didn't fully understand something, I'd hesitate. I'd nod along. I'd pretend I was tracking, just to avoid the embarrassment of being "the one who didn't get it." That moment of asking "Wait, can you explain that again?" felt too risky.

But over the years, I began noticing that the people I admired most—really smart, capable, high-level people, many of them men—would raise their hands or speak up and say, "I'm not following you. Can you explain that again?" They weren't trying to impress anyone. They were simply asking for clarity.

If they could admit they didn't understand something without shame or apology, why was I working so hard to pretend I understood? That realization helped me get over the hurdle. If someone I considered brilliant could say, "I don't get it," then I could too. In the process, I learned that speaking up doesn't diminish your credibility—it builds it.

To me, what power really looks like is the freedom to ask for clarity and the strength to admit you don't know something. It's having the confidence to speak the truth, even when it feels vulnerable.

I want you to experience that same freedom in your work and in your life—the freedom to be imperfect and to be a learner, not just a performer. When you stop pretending and start showing up fully and honestly, that's when real transformation begins.

It's not a flip of a switch. It's a process, but it's one you've already started. So take a breath. Raise your hand, and trust that your voice belongs in the room.

KEY TAKEAWAYS

- Creativity doesn't thrive under blanket pressure. Appropriately applied pressure—the kind that lifts up our ability to perform—is good. But creativity needs permission to get it wrong, to try something new, to be human and imperfect and still valuable.

- For so many women, the drive to be perfect and the need to be liked combine in dangerous ways. What if competence wasn't a mask we had to constantly maintain, but a well we could draw from? What if we didn't need a blue ribbon or a perfect review to validate growth? What if we believed, deeply and fully, that our mistakes didn't disqualify us but made us more competent?

- Enjoying your competence doesn't mean you expect things to go perfectly. It means you acknowledge how far you've come. You stop obsessing over the one thing you think you lack and start noticing all that you've built. That's the kind of freedom that comes when you stop waiting for someone else to tell you you're allowed, and you start giving yourself permission to show up as the skilled, growing, powerful woman you already are.

- Power is having the freedom to ask for clarity and the strength to admit you don't know something. It's having the confidence to speak the truth, even when it feels vulnerable. When you stop pretending and start showing up fully and honestly, that's when real transformation begins.

NINE

EARLY IMPRINTS AND SILENT RULES

THE MESSAGES WE RECEIVE GROWING UP, WHETHER explicit or implied, form our internal blueprints. We may not realize it as children, but those early imprints often become the silent rules we follow for decades.

In my case, the message was clear: *Be a good girl, the best girl. Don't make waves. Don't make trouble.* I didn't come to this conclusion through introspection as a child. It was a survival instinct in an unstable home. My father was volatile and unpredictable. His bipolar disorder was undiagnosed at the time, but his temper was explosive and terrifying. I learned quickly that to keep myself safe, I had to be perfect, nice, pleasing, and always composed.

There was no space for anger or rebellion, even in adolescence when those qualities naturally emerge. Instead of challenging my parents as many teens do, I tried to be the stabilizer, the fixer. My true feelings became secondary to maintaining peace and minimizing explosions.

I still remember one moment vividly. I was around fifteen and frustrated with my mom, who struggled with chronic depression and suicidal ideation. In a moment of exasperation, I said something mild by teenage standards: "You're just like so-and-so's mother," referencing someone we mutually disliked. It wasn't cruel, just a flare of honesty, but the result was catastrophic. My mother erupted, sobbing, threatening to kill herself, jumping into the car and driving off in a fury.

In that instant, the message of my childhood burned deeper into my being: My emotions were dangerous. I couldn't afford to be expressive, messy, or—God forbid—imperfect. Over time, that need to manage everyone else's reactions calcified into self-doubt. I questioned myself constantly. Was I too much? Too emotional? Too outspoken?

That internal caution, once a survival mechanism, became a cage.

As women, so often we learn early to shrink, to tiptoe, to silence parts of ourselves. Even when we're successful by all external measures, that fear of rocking the boat remains. This is one of the quiet tragedies I've witnessed over and over among my clients. Brilliant, capable women who still don't believe they have the right to take up space. They were never given permission to express their full selves, and they now mistake being "good" for being safe, even as their spirits yearn for something more.

Perhaps this resonates with you. If so, then I will tell you what I tell my clients—the healing begins when we recognize these patterns for what they are: old protective instincts that no longer serve us.

Looking back, I realize just how much I tiptoed around my own ambitions. I didn't recognize it at the time. Like so many of us, I was simply trying to make sense of the world and stay safe within it, but that delicate dance between striving and shrinking was deeply rooted in the complex environment I was raised in.

My mother was brilliant, but profoundly insecure. She carried a quiet, gnawing sense that she wasn't good enough, and I absorbed that message. I wanted to be like her because I admired her intelligence, strength, and beauty, but I also internalized her doubts. Without realizing it, I adopted the same unspoken belief: *There's something not quite right about me.*

She never said this out loud, of course, but the message came through all the same. I didn't grow up with the empowering voices so many of us long for: *You're amazing. Go out and do whatever you want. You're smart, you're strong, you're capable.* There's a quote by Dr. Seuss which resonated deeply with me when I first read it: "You have brains in your head. You have feet in your shoes. You can steer yourself in any direction you choose." That's the message I wish my mother had been able to give me. Instead, though, the underlying current was *be careful, don't get too big, don't trust your voice too much.*

My father, as I've said, was a tough litigator with a brilliant mind and an indomitable will, and despite his volatile temper, he taught me how to be strong in the world. Some of the fiercest battles of my life were with him. While I didn't go against him when I was younger, as I got older, I was often the only one who would challenge him, who would speak the truth no one else dared to say. That wasn't easy. As a litigator, he was trained to win arguments, but it gave me a kind of fortitude I wouldn't trade for anything. In learning to stand up to him, I learned how to stand up for myself.

He used to say something I'll never forget: "'No' is the first step to 'yes.'" I know not everyone loves that phrase, but it meant a lot to me. He was teaching me persistence and tenacity. He was saying, "Don't be discouraged by rejection. Don't take the first 'no' as final. Keep going." It's a lesson that's served me well—in business; in life; in the ring, on the back of a horse; and in the messy, complicated journey of healing.

The Power of Being Seen

Many of us receive mixed messages as children. My mother and father couldn't have been more different in the ways they navigated the world and projected their inner struggles. My father, despite his insecurities, used them as fuel. He pushed forward, fought hard, and played big. My mother, in contrast, carried a quieter, more inward self-doubt that dimmed her light.

My dad, for all his intensity, was someone I could argue with, and through that, I learned to speak up. That experience gave me grit, and it became a kind of emotional training ground. But not every woman has access to that dynamic. Not everyone grows up with someone who tells them, "You've got this. Go for it."

If you didn't have a parent or role model like that, it doesn't mean you're stuck. You can still build emotional resilience and grow your voice, but you might need to find those guiding figures outside your immediate family. I've spent much of my life doing exactly that, searching for the mother I didn't have. What I've learned is that the role of "mother" or mentor doesn't have to be filled by one person, or even by a woman. It can be many people over time. A mentor can be a friend, a coach, a trainer, a boss, or all of the above—someone who sees you clearly and calls out your strength.

We all need people who *see* us. Not just people who love us or support us in vague ways, but who truly recognize our potential and reflect it back to us. If you look closely at your life, there may already be someone who has seen you that way. It may be subtle, and it may not have lasted long, but it still matters. If you haven't had it yet, keep looking. It may not come in the form you expect, but that doesn't make it any less powerful.

As I reflect on my own mother, I realize that, for all the tragedies and doubts, she had her own quiet triumphs. She shined in her career and overcame considerable internal resistance to do so. Still, her chronic self-criticism and depression kept her from living as fully and joyfully as she could have. Her accomplishments were real, but so was her pain. I wish she could have had someone *see* her the way she deserved to be seen.

As for me, looking back, I now understand that I didn't feel truly seen by either of my parents—not fully. That recognition came later, pieced together from mentors, teachers, psychologists, and chosen family, but once it arrived, it changed my world. When someone finally sees you—really sees you—you start to see yourself differently too.

The Stories We Carry

I remember sitting in my first-grade classroom, bored out of my mind. This was old-school education: students reading aloud one by one, each of us holding our own copy of the book. I could already read fluently, but I had to sit quietly while the boy next to me painstakingly sounded out each word. I found myself flipping ahead, turning pages just to stay awake.

Eventually, the school recognized my advanced reading ability and bumped me up to second grade. But my grandmother, who had taught third grade in Michigan for over forty years, stepped in and said, "No, no, no, that's not a good idea. She can read, yes, but developmentally, she's still right where she belongs." And she was right. I had the intellect to skip ahead, but not necessarily the readiness and emotional maturity.

It was a rare instance of someone advocating for what was truly best for me, and it contrasts starkly with another story I was told as a child. My mother, at some point, told me I was of low-average intelligence. I carried that story with me for years and internalized it as truth. It became one of those painful stories that takes root in a young mind and blooms into decades-long self-doubt.

Later in life, as a trained psychologist, I came across my childhood psychological testing results from around fourth grade. I now understood how to interpret them, and you know what? My mother was very wrong. I wasn't low average—not even close. In fact, I had scored quite high on verbal intelligence, the part most correlated with traditional measures of IQ.

What had happened is that when I took the test, I was deeply depressed, and my performance score reflected that state. The result was a twenty-five-point gap between my verbal and performance scores, a disparity that indicates major emotional distress. Looking at those results as an adult, I felt both clarity and frustration. The testing psychologist had recommended psychotherapy for me, mentioning that I was depressed, anxious, and highly perfectionistic. Why didn't I get the help I needed at the time?

That misinterpretation of my test results became a lens through which I viewed myself for years. It reinforced the narrative that I was "less than," that I was somehow not enough. That's the danger of stories told to us by people who don't fully *see* us. Sadly, for many of us, those stories come early from the very people who are supposed to understand us the most.

Thankfully, over time, I've encountered people who *did* see me. My grandmother, for one, had the insight to step in when it mattered. My grandfather too, and later in life, mentors, psychologists, and trainers became mirrors for my potential. That's what we all need in our lives. Our healing begins when we start to surround ourselves with people who see our light even when we can't, and who gently return us to ourselves when our internal stories have led us astray.

When Labels Lie

It's a powerful thing to feel truly seen. I remember a time when a trusted trainer looked at me, met my nervous energy head-on, and said, point-blank, "Okay, I see you, and I see your anxiety too." That simple acknowledgment was profound. She didn't try to fix me or dismiss my fear. She just *saw* me, and in doing so, she gave me something many women crave but rarely receive: the sense that I could be whole, even with my messiness.

So often, we carry labels, either assigned by others or assigned by us. We get boxed in by phrases like "difficult," "anxious," "not that talented," or "not smart enough." These labels may be based on misunderstandings, or they may come from well-meaning people who simply couldn't see us clearly. Either way, once the label takes hold, it grows roots and becomes part of our internal narrative.

I've worked with riders who go through an objectively lovely round in the arena only to beat themselves up afterward because of one minor mistake. That single imperfection snowballs: *I blew it. I'm not a good rider. I'm failing. I can't do this.* They let their inner critic grab the mic, and it doesn't let go. This is how we shrink ourselves.

I spoke with a client recently who is a mother of two teenage daughters. One of them is the "rock star" athlete, naturally confident and praised for her performance. The other is a more sensitive, complex girl who's been labeled "different." She has learning differences, but she's also a vibrant, intuitive teenager struggling to be seen outside the diagnostic framework that's been built around her.

Her parents are loving and supportive, but they also operate in a high-achieving world. The moment anything seems "off," they assemble a team of specialists. I'm one of them, but I also try to offer perspective. When the mom called the other day, she was worried about a dramatic conflict between the girls. I listened to the details. It was just a blowup over something small.

"This is normal," I told the mother gently. "You have two teenage daughters. This is what it looks, sounds, and feels like."

The relief in her voice was immediate. I had helped her rip off the label. She realized it wasn't dysfunction or pathology. It was just the stormy weather of adolescence rolling through, and her job was to not crumble or overreact. To use a metaphor, she was to be the lighthouse, not the captain of the ship.

It reminded me of the time when my relatively minor comment to my mother, said in a moment of anger ("You're just like so-and-so's mom"), landed like a live grenade. I was fifteen and angry, but it was a throwaway comment. When my mother had a complete meltdown and threatened self-harm, it taught me a truly unfortunate lesson.

I needed her to hold space for my emotion—be the lighthouse when I was lost at sea—but she taught me by her reaction that anger, or at least the expression of anger, was dangerous. My emotions, no matter how sincere, could shatter people, so it was better not to express myself. After that, I began walking on eggshells because I'd internalized the idea that strong emotion, especially mine, was a threat.

What I needed was a mother who didn't absorb my pain as her own. I needed a calm response, or maybe a simple exit from the room—anything to show me that my big feelings weren't fatal.

As adults, unless we do the work to release them, we carry these old wounds around with us. Many of the women I work with struggle with their own versions of the same story. They accepted a label early in life, and it's still stuck to them. They say things like, "I'm just not that confident," or "I'm too sensitive," or "I've always been anxious." Maybe these labels were true at one time, but more often than not, they were never true at all, or they were a half-truth.

That's why an important part of our work is unlearning the old lessons. We have to drop the labels we've been carrying around and look instead at the facts of the situation. What we view as a character flaw might just be a regular part of life.

In doing this, we're not denying the struggle. We're reframing it in a way that enables us to show up more fully and more freely—in the saddle and in life.

Drop the Labels, Keep the Data

Too many women take an immediate leap from making a mistake to adopting a harsh identity label. For many of my clients, for example, a single misstep in the arena quickly becomes: *I'm a bad rider.* One tough round becomes: *That was a disaster.* When these thoughts go unchecked, they snowball into something much bigger than a single moment of disappointment. They become internal truths that shape how they see themselves not just in the ring, but in life.

I see this pattern so often that one of my core principles is to challenge this tendency. I always say, "Don't collapse a single moment into a sweeping judgment." So when a rider says "I'm bad" because they made a mistake, I'll respond by saying, "Wait. Let's think about this. You're a rider who made a mistake. And that mistake is not a character flaw. It's simply information we can use for the next round."

Then, we'll look at it. *What happened in that round? Why did the mistake occur?* By detaching the mistake from the label, we turn judgment into curiosity, and that's how we grow.

I like to remind clients that scientists never walk out of the lab saying, "I'm a bad scientist" when an experiment fails. If they did, they wouldn't be scientists for long. What do good scientists say instead? "Interesting. That's not the result I expected. What can I learn from this?"

Every failed experiment is just more data.

The moment we label ourselves, we box ourselves in. *Not good enough. Too anxious. Not cut out for this.* These are not facts. They are judgments, and judgment is the enemy of progress.

So much of the work I help my clients do is what I call "unlabeling," peeling away those limiting definitions we've absorbed from others or adopted ourselves. And it's critical work, because it's not just the label itself that's damaging, but the shame it invites. Labels aren't neutral—they carry emotional weight. For many women, especially those who grew up with perfectionist tendencies or unspoken expectations, those labels activate a deep sense of shame: *If I make a mistake, I must be bad. If I don't do everything perfectly, I must be failing.*

You can be flawed and worthy. You can be learning and still be powerful. You can make mistakes and still belong in the saddle. You are human, and you are enough.

Unlabeling doesn't mean ignoring what went wrong. It means examining it with compassion and clarity, so you can grow. You're not bad. You're not broken. You're just a scientist collecting data.

KEY TAKEAWAYS

- As women, so often we learn early to shrink, to tiptoe, to silence parts of ourselves. Even when we're successful by all external measures, that fear of rocking the boat remains. The healing begins when we recognize these patterns for what they are: old protective instincts that no longer serve us.

- Our healing begins when we start to surround ourselves with people who see our light even when we can't, and who gently return us to ourselves when our internal stories have led us astray.

- An important part of this work is unlearning the old lessons. Drop the labels you've been carrying around and look instead at the facts of the situation. What you view as a character flaw might just be a regular part of life. In doing this, you're not denying the struggle. You're reframing it in a way that enables you to show up more fully and more freely.

TEN

LET YOUR AMBITION ROAR

FOR MUCH OF MY LIFE, MY AMBITIONS LIVED IN A whisper. I kept them tucked away, hidden even from those closest to me. It's not that I lacked desire or direction, but I carried a strange, heavy shame around wanting more. I was afraid of what people might say.

Looking back, it feels bizarre. Now, in my role as a psychologist and mentor, I tell women and girls all the time, "Speak your dreams out loud. Ask. Reach out. Most people want to help." I welcome conversations with aspiring clinical or sport psychologists. I encourage my daughters—and my son—to ask for what they want and trust that someone will reach back.

The truth is, most people, especially those further along on the path, are more than willing to support someone coming up behind them.

I didn't believe that when I was younger. I thought if I showed my desire, someone would tell me I was asking for too much, or that I was not fit for my aspirations. I thought they would crush my dreams, so I kept quiet.

That fear impacted the way I moved through the world. I tiptoed around my goals.

Why did I feel the need to shield my ambition? Maybe it felt too vulnerable, or maybe it seemed presumptuous. I suppose I thought wanting something big would set me up for disappointment or make me a target for judgment.

There's nothing shameful about wanting more, but too many women are raised to please, to stabilize the emotional world around them. They quickly learn to shrink their dreams to make others comfortable. They bury their ambition so deeply it starts to feel like guilt.

If you're someone who's carried a dream in secret, afraid to say it out loud for fear of rejection or ridicule, you need to realize that generally the world is more welcoming than you think (and if someone doesn't support you, move on). Your ambition deserves daylight. Whether it's in the saddle, in your career, or in your heart, the first act of bravery is saying out loud, "I want this."

Let yourself say it. Then watch who shows up to help you rise.

Learning the Hard Way

As I tell my clients, the path to emotional clarity is never tidy. Sometimes it's tangled in memory, frustration, and the choices we make to define who we are and who we are *not*.

For me, one lesson came in the form of a battle with my father over working at our family's winery.

Chalk Hill Winery in Sonoma County was a sprawling project of ambition and vision—his and my stepmother's, not mine. As a young psychologist, I had no interest in grape varietals or cellar logistics. I had chosen a different path, in part as a rebellion. I didn't go to his alma mater or follow him into the law. I had earned my doctorate in psychology, was working through my postdoctoral training, and was busy preparing for my licensing exam. Psychology, not wine, was my world.

However, my dad wouldn't let it go. "You need to learn the business," he kept saying, as if it were some moral obligation. Eventually, I agreed to spend a year working there, figuring that at some point, the business might wind up in my lap, and I would be better off getting some experience with it.

Despite his words, my father seemed to have no plan for me to "learn the business." So, I wrote a proposal. I laid out exactly how I would spend my year: One quarter in the vineyard. One quarter learning the cellar operations. Another in sales and marketing. A fourth in finance, or whatever made sense at the time. I printed out my detailed four-page plan, prepared to discuss the ideas.

I walked into his office, nervous but proud. "Okay," I said. "I'll start on January 1. Here's how I propose we structure the year."

He took the pages, flipped through them without really looking, and then—without warning—ripped them in half.

"Who are *you* to write a plan?" he said. "You'll start in the cellar."

That was the dark side of him. The side that wanted control, the side that helped him win cases but could crush those closest to him.

I was furious, but I didn't fight back. Instead, I nodded and followed orders. I started in the cellar—the only member of my family to actually work there.

For eight long months, I worked side by side with the cellar crew, doing some of the most physically demanding labor of my life. Crawling between barrels and up on scaffolding to add sulfur, washing hundreds of bottles, lifting heavy equipment. I worked the bottling line, which was rote and ear-piercing and relentless. We had exactly two fifteen-minute breaks each day and a half hour for lunch. It was grueling, and it was isolating, except for one saving grace.

There was another woman in the cellar, a young attorney considering a leap into the wine business. We were both misfits in that world. We'd talk and laugh when we weren't supposed to, and the other workers would shake their heads at us every time we disrupted the rhythm of the bottling line. But she made it bearable.

By August, I had hit my limit. I had done the time and learned more than I ever wanted to about barrels and bottling, and I had also learned that I didn't need to prove anything anymore. I didn't need to do the job just because my father said I should, so I walked in and told him I was done. I was going to take my licensing exam, get my credentials, and continue my chosen, and earned, career.

Looking back, that year taught me more about identity than any course or client ever could. It taught me what happens when we trade our voice for approval and how painful and necessary it is to reclaim it. My father thought he was giving me an education in business, but really, I was learning something far more valuable: how to hold my ground.

My dad was many things: a brilliant lawyer, a charismatic entrepreneur, a man full of contradictions. He was both incredibly proud of me and fiercely competitive with me. He pushed me hard, expected strength, and often demanded submission, but in the same breath, he could express deep admiration. He wanted me to succeed but perhaps only in ways that didn't challenge him or disrupt the roles we had settled into.

I think, on some level, he was afraid of the parts of me that didn't fit his narrative, especially the parts that were strong and ambitious. That's one of the reasons why I was so quiet about what I really wanted for so long. I was afraid people would say, "You can't do that," or "Who do you think you are?" And my dad's voice—real or imagined—echoed loudest. And yet, paradoxically, it was also *because* of him that I felt I could be ambitious. He modeled drive. He built big things and showed me what it looked like to lead, even if I learned just as much from his missteps as from his successes.

Every woman I work with has a version of this story. Whether it's a father, a coach, a boss, or even an inner voice, there's a pressure to comply, to earn permission, to prove ourselves before we're allowed to take up space. But you don't need permission to chart your course. You don't need to suffer to prove your strength. Sometimes, the most powerful thing you can do is to walk out of the cellar, wipe the grit from your hands, and say, "This is not my path. I know who I am."

Don't shrink your ambition. Don't whisper your dreams. If you want something, say it out loud—to yourself and others. And if the voice in your head still says, "You're not allowed," ask yourself where that voice comes from. You may find it's not yours at all—and that you have the strength to silence it.

KEY TAKEAWAYS

- There's nothing shameful about wanting more. If you're someone who's carried a dream in secret, afraid to say it out loud for fear of rejection or ridicule, you need to realize that generally the world is more welcoming than you think (and if someone doesn't support you, move on). Your ambition deserves daylight.

- Every woman I work with feels a pressure to comply, to earn permission, to prove herself before she's allowed to take up space. But you don't need permission to chart your course. You don't need to suffer to prove your strength.

Sometimes, the most powerful thing you can do is stand up, wipe the grit from your hands, and say, "This is not my path. I know who I am."

- Don't shrink your ambition. Don't whisper your dreams. If you want something, say it out loud—to yourself and others.

ELEVEN

DISMANTLING THE "GOOD GIRL" IDENTITY

FOR MUCH OF MY LIFE, I BELIEVED THAT BEING "good" was not just admirable but necessary. I grew up needing to please, and I worked hard to be perfect, not because perfection felt fulfilling, but because I believed it kept me safe. If I was good enough, composed enough, responsible enough, maybe I could keep my family intact and peaceful.

There was always a part of me monitoring the room, quietly reading the emotions of others and adjusting accordingly. That hypervigilance didn't come from nowhere. I had a half brother who was a "squeaky wheel" in our family—he misbehaved, needed extra attention, and was often a cause for concern for my parents.

In response, as I've described, I decided: *I won't need anything. I'll be the best little girl ever.* I made being "low maintenance" a point of pride. The problem is, though, when you live your life trying not to need anything, you eventually lose sight of your own needs and boundaries. That "good girl" identity comes at a heavy cost.

In fifth grade, for example, I was placed in the back of the classroom, wedged between two notoriously disruptive (and irritating) girls. I always wanted to be in the front row, so it felt like a punishment. At first I didn't understand why the teacher sat me there; I was demoralized. When my mom asked about it, the school's response was simple: "Darby calms them down."

Darby settles the room. That was the role I'd been assigned. Not just by my family, but now by my school. The message was unspoken but clear: "It's your job to manage the emotions of others. Your goodness is a tool we can use to keep things peaceful."

Years later, that same dynamic replayed, this time with my daughter, Adele. Every year at her progressive, high-achieving school, she was grouped in class with the same three unruly boys. Finally, I asked the school why.

"Oh," they said, "Adele helps settle them down."

I thought, *Are you kidding? Forty years later, and we're still using quiet girls to manage unruly children.*

If you're like me, and like so many of the women I work with, you were raised to believe that asking for what you want is disruptive. That it makes you difficult. That you're worthy of love or respect only if you minimize your needs. But I want you to build the muscle of *self-advocacy* and say what you want. I want you to understand that being direct isn't the same as being rude, and that disruption, when rooted in truth, is often a gift.

This manifests in many ways, including some that are a bit silly. For example, if I go to a restaurant alone (or with my kids), I have noticed that sometimes I am seated at a less-desirable table. I'll wind up by the kitchen, or near the bathroom, or maybe in a dark corner. Sometimes this happens even if the place is empty.

Every time, I ask politely, "Excuse me, would it be possible to sit over there instead?"

You would not believe the looks I get. My kids get embarrassed. "Mom," they whisper, "you're being difficult."

No, I'm not. I'm not raising my voice or throwing a fit. I'm simply asking for what I want. Why does that feel so threatening? Why have we equated *self-expression* with *disruption*? Why do so many women feel the need to earn their space by first making themselves small?

These are questions we must continue to ask, not only in therapy rooms or coaching sessions, but in our daily lives.

Being good isn't the same as being whole, and no one can dim their light enough to hold the world together forever.

When Asking Feels Like Too Much

It's remarkable how something as simple as asking for a better table at a restaurant can become a microcosm of our entire inner world. These seemingly innocuous moments are rarely just about the table. They're about permission to prioritize our own needs without fearing that we're causing disruption.

If we struggle with something that small, what does that say about the bigger things? Of course we end up shrinking in our lives. Of course we hesitate to voice our needs or declare our ambitions. Somewhere along the line, we've absorbed the belief that speaking makes us look needy, rude, or worse, difficult.

I often say that all the roads in this work lead to the same place. Whether it's the harmful labels we internalize, the shame that keeps us quiet, or the sense that our presence is too much, it all stems from the same root: the fear of being seen and dismissed or even shamed.

Those moments at restaurants are deeply tied to an old memory. I was twenty-one years old, standing outside my professor's office at Cal (University of California, Berkeley). I remember wondering, *Can I ask him for a letter of recommendation? Can I tell him that I want to follow in his footsteps and pursue a doctorate? Or is that too bold? Will I look foolish? Entitled?*

I second-guessed my desire, and in doing so, I nearly passed on something that would largely determine the course of my life. I started to shrink myself. And now, years later, when I feel the hesitation to speak up and ask for a better table, I realize it's coming from the same place.

What's heartbreaking is how common this is, especially for women. These patterns don't arise out of nowhere. Many of us were raised to believe that speaking up was dangerous, or at least unseemly. We saw how women were criticized for advocating, while men were praised for it. We watched, often unconsciously, as our mothers were shushed, dismissed, or scolded for expressing themselves—while our fathers might be praised or admired for doing the exact same thing.

That double standard was evident in my youth, and now, decades later, I see it show up over and over again in the lives of the women I work with. Riders, professionals, mothers, daughters—it doesn't matter the context. The pattern is the same: *Be agreeable. Be accommodating. Be grateful for whatever seat you're offered. Be a good girl.*

No wonder it feels radical to say, "I'd like to sit over there, please."

But as hard as it is, there's something truly exciting about this. Because the moment we start speaking up is the moment we start to embrace our inner fire.

Start Where the Fire Is

One of my clients, a woman in her early thirties, is a professional horse trainer who is deeply committed to her craft. We've worked together for over three years, and I've seen her build her business from the inside out, laying groundwork in every area: relationships with clients, refining her skill in the arena, taking risks, trusting herself.

Lately, the seeds she's planted are finally blooming. Better clients are coming her way. She's placing well at bigger shows. Her owners are stepping up, offering to invest in higher-quality horses. From the outside, everything looks like it's finally falling into place. And yet, just the other night, she said something almost in passing that stopped me in my tracks: "I feel like an imposter."

We'd been talking about one of her favorite young horses. She'd trained and grown attached to this horse, but the owner wanted to sell him in order to upgrade to an even more talented horse. That emotional tug-of-war is something many professionals know all too well, but in this case, it was actually a moment of leveling up.

Her client wanted to invest in a top International Derby horse for her—one that had the ability to go to Derby Finals in Kentucky. My client was being given the opportunity to ride at that top level, but instead of feeling excited or proud, she sank into self-doubt.

"Am I just pretending I'm good enough to show a horse of that caliber?" she asked.

There it was. The imposter syndrome. That lurking fear that you're playing dress-up in someone else's boots because you don't truly belong. I could see where it was going. She was already talking about passing the ride to someone else. So I reminded her that discomfort in growth is not the same as fraud. You don't need to feel fully formed to take the next step. You don't need to be perfect to deserve the opportunity.

"Let's slow this down," I told her. "You say you want to be an

International Derby rider. You're not there yet, but you're on the path. That's not fraud. That's development. That's commitment."

And then I reminded her of her journey: the years of hard work, showing up when no one was watching, making tough calls, building her name. As I put it, "The fact that things are starting to click now doesn't make it overnight success. It's just the harvest finally arriving after a long season of sowing."

She said, "This is happening so fast." But that wasn't true. It just *looked* fast from the outside. Inside, it was the slow burn of resilience and vision.

The danger is that our labels shape our outcomes. If she kept calling herself an imposter, she would act like one. She'd give up the horse, question her ability, undermine herself in subtle ways until others might start to doubt her too.

This is why we must examine the names we give ourselves. "Not good enough." "Too ambitious." "A fraud." "Just lucky." These are not just passing thoughts. They are invitations to self-betrayal.

I told her, and I'll tell you: *You're not an imposter. You're becoming*. That's the work. And you know what? If that journey feels uncomfortable, stirs doubt, or makes you question your place, it means you're on the right track.

The Courage to Want More

When I think about what holds so many talented women back, it's not a lack of skill or work ethic. It's the fear of being seen as *too much*. Too ambitious. Too intense. Too serious.

That client who is being offered an International Derby mount is on the verge of a major breakthrough in her riding career. That elite-level horse will put her in top-tier territory. Instead of celebrating, though, she began questioning herself. "What if I'm not good enough? What if someone else should ride this horse?"

She was even prepared to step aside and hand the ride to someone else. If she gives the ride away, and that other rider wins, it will become confirmation of her doubt. "See? They won because they're better than I am." Her story then becomes self-fulfilling.

But if she says yes and rides through the discomfort, trusts herself, and claims her place, then she will grow. Even if she makes a mistake, she will be closer to the rider, and the woman, she's meant to be.

That's how we become unshrinkable. Bear in mind, this client once told me that her goal is *world domination*. When she said it, I didn't flinch. Instead, I replied, "Well then, we better get you a world-domination horse." We laughed, but we both knew it was more than a joke. It was a declaration and a refusal to hide her ambition.

I hold her ambition with her. That's part of our work together. I want to remind her—and every woman I work with—that ambition is not a liability. Ambition tells us where we're meant to go.

Her husband, too, offered encouragement. He told her, "You've got to lift your eyes up." And he was right. We can't claim our future if we're always looking down, second-guessing, apologizing for wanting more.

There's a quiet, cultural undercurrent that teaches women to conceal their ambition. I've experienced it firsthand. Throughout my life, people have said to me, "You're so serious," as if that were a flaw. Not "You're so passionate" or "You're so dedicated," but *serious*—like it's something I should hide.

For a long time, I wondered: *Is that bad? Am I too much?* But ambition isn't something to be ashamed of. It's a kind of internal compass that tells us what matters, and when we honor it, we give other women permission to do the same.

So if you've ever been called too serious, too driven, too intense—good for you. That means you're exactly where you're supposed to be.

The real work is learning to *own* your ambition. To say, "Yes, I want this," without apology.

> **There's a profound shift that happens when a woman stops apologizing for her ambition and starts owning it. When she stops qualifying her passions and allows herself to show up fully as the powerful, competent, high-achieving person she already is.**

"Just Dabbling"

I have one client—we talked a little about her earlier in the book—who is a high-level executive. In her professional life, she's exceptional. She is respected, accomplished, and responsible for big outcomes. But she still struggles with her ambition, both in her professional life and her riding life. When it comes to riding, she'll downplay her goals, joke about her horse being *just* a Thoroughbred, or shrug off her dressage aspirations as "just dabbling."

This same woman has invested in a fancy horse, shows up consistently, and rides with precision and intention. She's competitive and wants to win, yet admitting that—even to herself—has been a struggle. For a while, she wouldn't let herself buy the high-end clothing brands that many dressage riders wear, because to her, that would mean saying, "I'm a real dressage rider." She didn't want to seem presumptuous.

Over time, we worked through it. We talked about how the way we identify matters. If you see yourself as a "real" rider, you start to ride like one. You care for your horse differently. You show up to your workouts with more clarity. You wear the breeches not to impress anyone else, but to signal to yourself: *This is who I am.*

This attitude extended beyond the arena. Remember earlier when we talked about how our self-language matters? She's also a runner and has been for years, but she constantly called herself "just a runner." Never an athlete. I challenged her: "If you think of yourself as an athlete, you will make decisions that athletes make. That means you prioritize rest and nutrition. You will train consistently, and most importantly, you will own your truth."

Weeks later, she told me something beautiful. After a 10K race, she looked me in the eye and said, "Darby, I really felt that I was a runner. An athlete." The way she held herself had changed. She wasn't pretending anymore. She was simply acknowledging what had already been true.

That's my invitation for every woman who feels the tug of something more. You don't need to wait for someone to validate your ambition. You don't need to win a ribbon or prove a point to own what lights you up. You just have to say yes to your drive and your goals, and then show up as the person you already are.

Notice What's Going On

Whether we realize it or not, the stories we tell about who we are and what we're capable of become the ceiling of our own lives. The beautiful part is that we can rewrite those stories.

Before we can do that, however, we have to *notice what's going on*. That may sound simple, but in my experience—both as a psychologist and a rider—it's one of the hardest things for people to do. Our self-talk and doubts tend to run on autopilot. We don't question the stories we tell ourselves because they've become so familiar, so habitual, that we stop even realizing they're there.

That's why, in my work with clients, one of the most powerful first assignments I give is this: *Just notice. I'm not asking you to change anything yet. Just notice. Notice every time you qualify your ambition. Notice when you downplay your goals or talk yourself out of being a "real" rider, athlete, or competitor. Notice the language you use to describe yourself, your horse, your work, your value.*

Once you start noticing, the change has already begun.

This exercise unfolded beautifully with that high-level executive. As you know, when we first started working together, she wouldn't even admit to herself that she was ambitious. In fact, she'd go out of her way to deny it.

She had plenty of drive but also a deep-seated fear of being perceived as "superior." In her family, ambition wasn't something you proudly wore. It was something you kept hidden. Like so many of my younger clients, she didn't want to seem like she thought too much of herself.

The change began by gently encouraging her to notice—just notice—these patterns. Over time, the self-talk changed. She went from "I'm just dabbling," to "I'm a dressage rider." Not a "dressage rider riding a Thoroughbred." Not "someone who tries hard." A bona fide, competent dressage rider.

That seemingly small shift in identity changed everything, because how you identify determines how you show up.

When you believe you're an athlete, you train like one and recover like one. When you believe you're a serious rider, you start making decisions that reflect that belief. You ride with more presence and purpose.

So wherever you are on your journey, start by noticing. That's the inroad. Create even a sliver of space between your automatic thoughts and your conscious awareness. Once you do, you can begin to own your ambition, your identity, your voice.

You are allowed to want more, and you don't need to apologize for it.

Holding Ambition Until You're Ready

I've had the same struggle myself. When I first started building my current business, I was hesitant and unsure. I was lured into playing small and not fully owning what I was building. There were some people around me who seemed skeptical, as if they were expecting me to fail. That kind of energy can seep in and feed the self-doubt already bubbling beneath the surface.

A consultant I worked with at the time saw me clearly. She didn't tiptoe around my insecurities. Instead, she simply said, "You are a psychologist. You work in sport and performance. You're already doing it and doing it well. Own it. Use the title. Stop diminishing yourself." There was no fluff, no hand-holding—just clarity and confidence.

It was like she picked up a riding crop and said, "Forward. Go. We're jumping this." And I listened. I'm still grateful to her.

She embraced my ambition when I was still unsure of myself. She gave me permission to step into the identity I had been quietly crafting. In that moment, she did for me what I now do for my clients: She lifted my eyes toward the horizon and said, "That's where you're going. I can see it, even if you can't yet."

That kind of mentorship is powerful. It's far more than mere encouragement. It's about seeing someone's potential and refusing to let them shrink away from it. It's about holding someone's ambition with both hands until they're confident enough to hold it themselves.

I want to do that for you, especially if you don't have anyone else who is willing to do so. With this book, I am saying, "I see you. I see what you want, even if you're not saying it yet. And I will not let you shrink." You may not feel ready to show up fully in your riding or your life. That's okay. I'll hold the vision for you until you can carry it yourself.

We all need someone to do that for us. Whether it's a coach, a mentor, a psychologist, or even a trusted friend who calls out your shrinking act, we all need a mirror that reflects not just who we are but who we *could* be.

That isolating feeling that you're the *only one* who wrestles with self-doubt? I hear it from women all the time. They believe they're alone in their fear and hesitation. They think everyone else has it figured out, but the truth is, these feelings are very common and also deeply private. They thrive in silence.

That's one of the purposes of this book—and why I've shared my own story within it. Part of this work is simply saying, "You're not alone." You're not the only one who's ever struggled to claim the title of "athlete," or "rider," or "leader." You're not the only one who's ever bought the fancy horse and then questioned whether you deserved it. And you're definitely not the only one who's ever wanted to dream bigger while secretly wondering if it's okay to want more.

So let me say what maybe no one has yet said to you: It is okay to want more. It is more than okay to be ambitious. If you're not ready to say it out loud just yet—*I am driven, I am competent, I am ambitious*—then let me say it for you for now. Until you're ready to ride forward and claim it for yourself.

KEY TAKEAWAYS:

- I want you to build the muscle of self-advocacy and say what you want. I want you to understand that being direct isn't the same as being rude, and that disruption, when rooted in truth, can be a gift.

- Being good isn't the same as being whole, and no one can dim their light enough to hold the world together forever.

- The moment you start speaking up is the moment you start to embrace your inner fire.

- If you feel the tug of something more, you don't need to wait for someone to validate your ambition. You don't need to win a ribbon or prove a point to own what lights you up. You just have to say yes to your drive and your goals, and then show up as the person you already are.

- The stories we tell about who we are and what we're capable of become the ceiling of our own lives. The beautiful part is that we can rewrite those stories. Before we can do that, however, we have to notice what's going on. That may sound simple, but in my experience—both as a psychologist and a rider—it's one of the hardest things for people to do. Our self-talk and doubts tend to run on autopilot. That's why, in my work with clients, one of the most powerful first assignments I give is this: Just notice. I'm not asking you to change anything yet. Just notice. Notice every time you qualify your ambition. Notice when you downplay your goals. Notice the language you use to describe yourself, your work, your value. Once you start noticing, the change has already begun.

TWELVE

WRANGLING SELF-CRITICISM

SO OFTEN, WHEN WOMEN COME TO ME—WHETHER they're teenage athletes or accomplished professionals in their fifties—they are burdened with the same underlying fear: *Am I the only one who feels this way?* They don't realize that other riders, other professionals, or even other mothers wrestle with the same doubts, insecurities, and fears. They've convinced themselves their pain is uniquely theirs. But after decades of doing this work, I can say unequivocally that while every person's experience is certainly personal, the emotions underneath are universal.

Isolation is a powerful force. It magnifies self-doubt, breeds shame, and convinces us that everyone else is somehow breezing through life while we're stuck in the muck of self-questioning. That's why one of the first things I do with a client is normalize their experience.

I might say something like, "I was just talking to someone earlier today who's wrestling with a very similar fear," or "This reminds me of a teenager I spoke with this morning." I never share names or personal details, of course, but I intentionally weave in these echoes of similarity so they can begin to feel the connection.

We humans tend to isolate ourselves in our pain. We believe we're uniquely flawed, but isolation lies to us. It tells us we don't belong. But when you realize that others share your struggles—that they too question their worth, or their right to ambition—it softens the shame. It may even open the door to insight.

When I offer those little examples—"You know, I worked with someone just this morning who was struggling with something similar"—it's a way to say: Others have come through it, and so can you.

When my husband recently underwent cutting-edge surgery, the surgeon reassured us, "I've done this two hundred times before." Even though the procedure was new and rare, that level of experience gave us confidence to move forward. We knew we were in capable hands.

It's the same with therapy and healing. When I say, "Yes, I've seen this pattern before," I'm not dismissing your experience. I'm inviting you to trust the process. I'm saying, "You are not alone and you can get through this too."

It's not a magic cure, but it can help loosen the grip that shame or self-doubt has on you. And once that loosens, growth can begin.

I want you to hear me clearly: *You are not the only one*. You're not the only one who doubts your worth, who hides ambition, or who fears taking up space, and you're not the only one who can learn to change that.

I've worked with women of all ages, and while their contexts differ, their vulnerabilities often look the same. Whether it's a seventeen-year-old who's afraid to express her ambition or a fifty-year-old who's been hiding her dreams for decades, what they're feeling underneath is the same: fear of being seen and shamed, fear of standing out, fear of not being enough.

Teenagers, especially, are developmentally wired to feel this self-consciousness. I see it all the time. When I dropped my daughter off at college for her freshman year, every single nineteen-year-old looked exactly the same—same shorts, same tank top, same slightly anxious posture. Fitting in feels safer than standing out, and at that time in their lives, the need to fit in is developmentally appropriate. At that age, they're still figuring out who they are. They're trying on identities—intellectual, athlete, artist, maybe even rebel—until something feels right.

The process of trying on identities isn't exclusive to college kids. Many women I work with are still doing it, even decades later. They're just doing it more quietly—testing out if they can claim the title of "athlete" or "leader" or "ambitious rider" without feeling selfish or fake. They're asking, "Am I allowed to want more?"

Yes, you are. So if you're reading this and thinking, "But my fears are different," I want to challenge you. The details may differ, but the core is the same. You're not the only one. You're not behind. You're not broken.

The process of stepping into that truth isn't instantaneous, but if you're reading this and wondering whether you're the only one who feels this way, I want you to know that you are not. You're already on the path to discovery.

You're good as you are. Exactly as you are in this moment—not who you'll become one day, not once you've earned more ribbons, gained more clients, or achieved some elusive status. You are already enough. That doesn't mean you won't grow. The practitioner I was ten years ago is not the practitioner I am today. I wasn't lacking then, and you're not lacking now. You're in the process, doing the work, and that means you're exactly where you need to be.

This truth applies to the Fortune 500 executive sitting at the head of the table, the mom starting her own business, or the woman preparing for a clinic with butterflies in her stomach. The message is the same: *You can hold your own. You can take up space. You belong.*

It's tempting to forget that. We live in a world that thrives on judgment and comparison. Whether it's grades, rankings, social media, or even casual conversations with friends or colleagues, we're constantly measuring ourselves against others or against the version of us we think we *should* be.

From Self-Judgment to Self-Evaluation

Just recently, my daughter came home from college and said, "Mom, everyone gets A's now." Of course, not *everyone* gets A's, especially not at a place like the University of Michigan, but the people she spends time with, the ones she compares herself to, are all top performers.

That's what judgment does. It tells us we're not enough. It insists that we need to be better, prettier, smarter, more accomplished, more something, and nowhere is that louder than on social media, where the highlight reel of everyone else's life plays on repeat.

I see the impact most clearly in my younger clients who scroll through carefully curated images and feel, somehow, that they're not enough or that they don't measure up. Frankly, adults aren't much better. We may pretend we're more immune to it, but many of us are quietly drowning in the same feelings. I've even told some of my clients, especially those struggling with self-worth, to limit their social media use, because when the comparison becomes constant, it can be soul-crushing.

The women I work with aren't lounging around and waiting for life to happen. They are driven, successful, and hungry for more, and precisely because of that, they often feel the pressure more intensely. They get lost in comparison with others, not to mention with some kind of imaginary ideal of what or who they should be.

That voice is judgment, and it thrives in silence. So let's bring it into the open. Let's acknowledge that comparison is a normal part of the human experience, but it doesn't have to define us. We can hold space for our ambition without letting judgment crush us. We can honor the work of others without diminishing our own. We can look in the mirror and say, "I am good as I am. I still want to be better, but I don't need to diminish myself in order to grow."

Self-judgment is often wrapped up with competitiveness, perfectionism, envy, and the constant drive to prove ourselves. But this isn't a valid self-evaluation. This is harsh, emotional, often irrational judgment, which derails performance just as fast as a missed cue. The most successful people I work with tend to be the hardest on themselves. Their ambition is part of what drives their excellence. But when that drive turns inward with cruelty instead of clarity, it becomes self-sabotage.

It's not that self-evaluation is wrong. In fact, it's essential for growth. You need to be able to assess what's working and what isn't if you're going to step into your fullest potential, but this helpful instinct to self-reflect gets hijacked by perfectionism and self-judgment.

Women, in particular, tend to make it personal. Instead of "That transition was a little off," it becomes "I'm a failure." Men, in my experience, are generally better at separating performance from identity, but my female clients tend to go straight to blanket pressure, as we discussed earlier.

I teach something different. I encourage my clients to focus on today. You must still hold the big vision while staying grounded in the moment. What do you want to accomplish today given the reality of what you are working with? Are you tired? Have you just gotten some bad news? Are you at the beginning of your career? That context matters.

When you're in the arena, there's no room for judgment. Not the good kind, and not the bad kind. You don't have time to pat yourself on the back or tear yourself down. The focus must be in the moment. That's where the ride happens.

And then, after the ride, we evaluate, but we do it in a way that's *specific* and constructive. "I felt more connected in our lateral work." "I kept my shoulders quiet." Or "I lost focus in the last half, and that's something I want to work on next time." That kind of reflection is useful. It gives you data you can work with.

For example, if your horse dropped behind you and you overcorrected with too much leg, say exactly that: "I used too much leg." That's a technical observation, not an emotional response. We need to train our minds to be more "workmanlike" or objective—to avoid the emotional and global self-criticism that says, "I'm a failure. I shouldn't even be here."

Keep Working the Process

One of my clients recently shared a story about working with her trainer to keep her hands soft when her horse gets tense. He's the kind of horse who can go from zero to sixty in an instant, and she tended to become rigid and defensive as a way to prevent an escalation. But her tension only made things worse. So now, when she feels that anxiety creep in, she focuses on her breath. That's the kind of growth we celebrate. Not "Did I nail every movement perfectly?" but rather "How well did I respond to what I was working on today?"

I don't let my clients use global words like *bad* when describing their performance. "It was a bad ride or bad presentation" tells me nothing. Did you fall off? Did your horse spook? Did you forget what you were going to say? Did your plan get derailed? I need to know what actually happened. More importantly, *you* need to know what actually happened. The point of being specific is to be workmanlike about your feedback, not emotional. Saying "My performance was bad" is a blanket judgment, and it tells me nothing. Besides, it's highly unlikely that every part of your performance was bad.

The same goes for "good." Don't tell me it was a good ride or a good meeting. Tell me what *worked*. What felt better. What you want to build on next time. You need to know about the successful parts too, and learn from and savor those. Remember, you're not a bad rider because your horse acted up. You're not a bad speaker because you made a mistake in your presentation. You're a human who is evolving, and the only way to grow is to let go of the perfectionism, define success for *this* moment, and keep working the process.

That is not lowering the bar. That is how you get better—in the ride, and in your life.

KEY TAKEAWAYS

- Many women don't believe that other people wrestle with the same doubts, insecurities, and fears. They've convinced themselves their pain is uniquely theirs. If you've struggled with isolation too, I want you to hear me clearly: You are not the only one. You're not the only one who doubts your worth, who hides ambition, or who fears taking up space, and you're not the only one who can learn to change that.

- Self-judgment is often wrapped up with competitiveness, perfectionism, envy, and the constant drive to prove ourselves. But this isn't a valid self-evaluation. This is harsh, emotional, often irrational judgment, and it derails performance just as fast as a missed cue. It's not that self-evaluation is wrong. You need to be able to assess what's working and what isn't if you're going to step into your fullest potential, but this helpful instinct to self-reflect gets hijacked by perfectionism and self-judgment. That's why I encourage you to focus on today. Hold the big vision, but bring it back to what you want to accomplish in this moment, given the reality of what you are working with right now.

THIRTEEN

RECLAIMING YOUR IDENTITY

OUR IDENTITY SHAPES HOW WE WALK THROUGH the world. It defines not just how we think about ourselves, but how we show up and what we allow ourselves to pursue, want, and become. For many of the women I work with, the question of identity is both powerful and tender. I see it in the riders who are rediscovering the strength they had as competitors decades ago, and I've felt it deeply in my own life too. There was a period when I stepped back from my daily professional work to raise my family. It was something I chose, something I cherished, yet something about it left me feeling incomplete.

I didn't stop being a psychologist during those years. I wasn't seeing clients every day, but the identity didn't disappear. It went quiet. It slipped to the background, but I missed it. I missed the parts of me that had taken years of education, training, and effort to build. I missed the lens through which I'd always made sense of the world.

Becoming a mother gave me a new and beautiful identity, but it didn't replace the old one. I came to realize that motherhood alone, though deeply meaningful, didn't fully encompass who I was. I never stopped being a mother, but I also never stopped being a psychologist. That part of me was no longer being nourished, but the longer I went without feeding it, the more adrift I felt. I needed both, and I had to find ways to bring my psychologist self back into my life as an active part of my being.

So, I got creative. I joined several nonprofit boards. I volunteered my expertise. I taught classes for parents and teachers. I became a consultant for several preschools and for a therapeutic equestrian center. While I didn't return to full-time private practice immediately, I needed to feel like I was contributing professionally—like I was still *me*.

I've seen this same tug-of-war play out in the lives of my clients. Whether it's a rider reconnecting with the part of her that once competed at the highest level, or a woman in her fifties who's finally allowing herself to say, "I'm still ambitious," these identity shifts matter. They're about acknowledging the whole of who we are and making space for every piece.

When we disconnect from a core part of ourselves, we can

lose our way. Sometimes, the most healing thing we can do for ourselves is to find our way back.

Internalizing Limiting Beliefs

Remember my client who hesitated to take the ride on the talented Derby horse? When she questioned whether she was worthy of riding and showing that horse, she was playing out an internal limiting belief. After all, her client saw and believed in her talent! All the doubt was in her own mind.

When we internalize limiting identities, they become the framework through which we interpret every experience. And unless we challenge that narrative, our choices will continue to validate it. When we decide to step into a bigger identity, even before we feel fully "ready," it changes how we train, how we ride, and how we handle setbacks. It gives us permission to grow into the person and athlete we truly want to become.

Sometimes, the biggest breakthroughs don't happen in the arena—they happen in how we see ourselves. I've watched equestrians transform not just their riding but their entire lives by shifting their own self-identity.

One of my clients is a seasoned dressage professional in her mid-forties. When we first started working together several years ago, her business was riddled with compromises. She undercharged, accepted clients who treated her poorly, and wore herself out trying to make everyone happy. At the heart of it all was a core belief she had carried for years: *I can make a silk purse out of a sow's ear.*

In her mind, her greatest strength was her ability to take an average, overlooked horse, maybe even a broken one, and turn it into something remarkable. In many ways, that was true. She had a gift for seeing potential and making the most of difficult situations, but this identity had become a trap. She'd built a career on proving she could succeed with less, which kept her stuck in cycles that limited her growth.

The truth is that she didn't want to ride fixer-uppers. She dreamed of Grand Prix arenas, fancy warmbloods, and high-level partnerships, but her self-image—this identity she clung to—kept her from stepping fully into that dream.

We worked on this over the months and years, and step by step, she began to reimagine who she was. She let go of the scrappy underdog role and started identifying as the rider she truly wanted to be: a top-level professional. Today, she runs a high-caliber barn, sells quality warmbloods, and competes successfully at the most prestigious horse shows. Her life changed when her identity did.

I see the same challenge in younger women too. One of my clients, a bright and talented twenty-five-year-old hunter/jumper trainer, struggled to see herself as a "real" professional. She wanted to be liked, to keep her clients happy, but that desire blurred the lines of her role and made it hard for her to assert herself.

In one session, she told me about a horse in her program who was showing signs of pain. The owner didn't want to spend any more money on veterinary care and insisted the horse should still compete. My client knew this wasn't right, but didn't know how to speak up. She was torn between being nice and being responsible.

I told her, "Step into your role as a professional. When you're the expert, your first responsibility is to the horse, and as a professional, it's not just your right to speak up, it's your duty." I reminded her that every expert in our lives—whether it's a plumber, an attorney, or a physician—has the responsibility to deliver the truth, even when it's inconvenient or uncomfortable.

This is the key distinction. When you step fully into your professional identity, the rules change. You're no longer just a friend or a people-pleaser. You become the voice of wisdom, the trusted authority your clients need, and that requires courage.

However, for this young woman—and for many others I work with—there's a conflict between wanting to be seen as kind and fearing that authority will make them unlikable. This is a false choice.

> **True leadership doesn't require you to abandon compassion. True leadership requires you to embrace clarity and responsibility.**

So many women experience a tension between how they *see* themselves and what they're *called* to become. Much of my work is helping riders and professionals step into the identity that matches their ambition—not the one shaped by insecurities or outdated roles.

When we reject limiting, internalized self-beliefs and embrace our honest, ambitious identity, it changes our behavior, and everything else follows.

When Being "Nice" Holds You Back

This leads me to one of the most common and damaging patterns I see in the women I work with, regardless of their identity: the compulsion to be *nice*. It often starts young, as part of the social programming many of us grew up with: *Don't make waves. Put others first.*

But when this people-pleasing mindset creeps into professional life, it can have serious consequences. Many of my clients are compassionate, capable, driven women who hold themselves back without fully realizing it. They fear losing a client, so they avoid hard conversations. They downplay their expertise to make others feel comfortable. They allow subpar clients, horses, or working conditions to remain because they're afraid to say no.

When we operate out of fear—fear of being unliked, fear of losing business, fear of being too authoritative—we attract relationships that keep us stuck. But when we show up in full alignment with our values, we invite the right people in.

Another client—a forty-two-year-old professional—recently experienced this identity shift writ large. When we first started working together, her barn was filled with clients who drained her. She undercharged, overworked, and constantly doubted herself. One of her clients was a particularly difficult man who was frustrating to teach, bargained her down to half price, and even then did not pay on time.

She was miserable. She knew she was being taken advantage of. And yet—like so many of us—she struggled to make changes. Why? Because of the story she told herself: *I feel bad for the horse.* But by staying in an unhealthy situation out of guilt or obligation, she was sacrificing her own well-being—and that of her business.

Her acceptance of these working conditions was symptomatic of the fact that she was allowing herself to be diminished. And she was suffering for it—financially, emotionally, and energetically. She tolerated it all, believing this was simply who she was. She identified as someone who made things work, no matter how unreasonable the situation.

She paid a heavy price for that identity, including financial instability, constant stress, and a barn filled with clients who didn't align with her long-term goals. It wasn't until she began challenging that identity, questioning whether she actually *wanted* to be the go-to trainer for impossible situations, that things began to shift. She started letting go of clients who drained her.

Once she began to shift her identity, to think of herself as "the high-level professional with high standards," she started attracting more serious clients, raised her rates, and created boundaries that honored her time and expertise. Her business grew, and so did her peace of mind. The difficult man she dreaded teaching left her program and found another trainer better suited to his style—someone who *liked* answering forty questions per lesson. He was happier, and so was she.

These kinds of transformations begin with a single decision to stop diminishing ourselves and to start stepping into a truer, bolder identity. Every time we shrink ourselves in the name of being "nice," we send a message to the world and to ourselves that we're not worth more.

You can be compassionate *and* authoritative. You can be caring *and* clear. You can speak the truth, advocate for yourself, uphold your standards, *and* still be respected, even loved. In fact, that's where real respect begins.

The stories you tell yourself *about* yourself are the foundation that shapes your experiences. If you believe that your worth comes from being endlessly accommodating, you'll struggle to say no. You'll feel guilty when you do.

When we shift our internal narrative, we change what and who we attract. Remember, what we believe about ourselves determines how we show up in the world, and how we show up determines who and what we invite in.

So what kind of person do you want to be known as? And what kind of life are you willing to build to support that vision?

Leveling Up Without Apology

Growth often comes with unexpected guilt. Recently, one of my long-term clients came to me with a dilemma. She was about to make a major move, both literally and symbolically. After years of hard work, she had the opportunity to relocate her business to a shared property with her longtime mentor. The new facility would elevate everything: her program, her visibility, her clientele, and most importantly, her identity.

She was stepping into the next chapter of her professional life, and it was a beautiful, hard-earned leap forward. Instead of celebrating, though, she was tangled up in anxiety over having to tell the current barn owner she was leaving.

"I just feel bad," she told me. "She's done a lot for me."

So I asked, "What, specifically, has she done?"

"Well, we've exchanged training tips. I once borrowed a bridle from her, but I gave her two pairs of gloves in return. She's worked hard to keep the barn running, I guess."

It became clear that while the current barn owner had done her job, she hadn't gone above and beyond in any unusual way. Still, my client felt she owed her something. In reality, she was struggling with a sense of guilt for leveling up.

As women, many of us have been taught to avoid making others uncomfortable, even at our own expense. Saying goodbye, even in a professional setting, can feel like betrayal. The underlying thought is rarely spoken aloud but often deeply felt: *Who am I to move up when you're still here?*

This is business, and more importantly, this is growth. So I helped her rehearse what to say: "I want to let you know I'll be moving on. I've found a new opportunity that's a great fit for me and my clients. I've really appreciated being here and everything you've done to support me this past year. Thank you so much."

That's it. Clear, kind, and professional. She nodded, feeling the relief of having a script to follow, but the guilt still lingered.

"What if she says, 'I wish you'd told me last week. I had someone who wanted your spot'?" my client asked.

"That would be unprofessional," I replied. "What she *should* say is, 'I'm happy for you, and I'll miss having you here.' Anything else is about her, not about you."

That was a light bulb moment. She realized that the real discomfort wasn't about the logistics of leaving. It was about *leaving someone behind*. The emotional unease wasn't rooted in what her landlord had done for her but what moving forward symbolized. It felt like she was saying, "I'm going to the next level, and I'm not bringing you with me."

Sometimes, success feels hard because it separates us. For women who've been conditioned to maintain harmony, that separation feels like a wound we're not supposed to cause.

But we must remember that rising isn't abandonment. It's okay to outgrow spaces, situations, and relationships that no longer serve our highest vision. There is no need to apologize for leveling up. Don't shrink to make others comfortable. Step up and don't look back.

I see this conflict across every age and discipline. What helps us overcome this guilt is having a solid identity that isn't fragile. This is why I encourage my clients to step fully into the identity they *want* to create.

You want to be a great athlete? Then walk, speak, and think like one. Want to be a respected executive? Embrace it. Once you fully adopt the identity, you are on your way. There is no waiting. The stronger your identity, the more confident and resilient you become. You'll no longer be defined by the highs and lows of a single ride or client interaction. And you won't be racked with guilt when you finally achieve something you've been working hard to accomplish.

Voices from Outside

Sometimes, the biggest enemy to our ambitious identity is our own internal self-criticism, but other times, the doubting voices come from the outside world. I've seen this dynamic firsthand in my own life. Years ago, you'll recall, when I was pursuing psychoanalytic training, I was told by someone I deeply respected in the field that psychologists rarely became psychoanalysts. The path was more common for psychiatrists. Fortunately, I didn't buy into that limitation. I didn't let the world define what I could or couldn't do. I pursued it anyway, and I became both—a psychologist and a psychoanalyst.

Not everyone has that kind of internal resistance to imposed identity. Some do absorb the limitations others place on them.

One client in her thirties comes to mind. She's a smart, capable horse trainer, living a life she loves, but her parents have a different vision for her life. They're from an affluent suburb outside of New York, steeped in traditional ideals, steady jobs in finance, country clubs, kids in private school. Her siblings all followed that path, but she didn't. She chose horses.

To her parents, her career doesn't quite "count." It's unpredictable and doesn't fit the mold. They continually encourage her to settle down, to do something more "normal," more "respectable," and even though she's rebellious enough to reject their plan, that lingering pressure still pulls at her. She wonders if maybe they're right

That contrast between *who we know we are* and *what others want us to be* can create deep identity conflict. The key is alignment. When we aren't aligned with our core identity, everything feels harder.

True power comes from clarifying who we are and showing up accordingly. When identity and action match, we stop apologizing for who we are. We stop tolerating disrespect, and we start building the kind of careers and lives that reflect our deepest values and aspirations.

So yes, how you identify matters, but even more important is making sure that identity is truly yours—not one that's been handed to you, imposed on you, or politely accepted out of guilt or obligation. When you step into the identity that feels true, a world of potential opens up before you.

KEY TAKEAWAYS

- When we internalize limiting identities, they become the framework through which we interpret every experience. And unless we challenge that narrative, our choices will continue to validate it. When we decide to step into a bigger identity, even before we feel fully "ready," it gives us permission to grow into the person we truly want to become.

- When we operate out of fear—fear of being unliked, fear of losing business, fear of being authoritative—we attract relationships that keep us stuck. But when we show up in full alignment with our values, we invite the right people in.

- Every time we shrink ourselves in the name of being "nice," we send a message to the world and to ourselves that we're not worth more. You can be compassionate and firm. You can be caring and clear. You can speak the truth, advocate for yourself, uphold your standards, and still be respected, even loved. In fact, that's where real respect begins.

- The stories you tell yourself about yourself are the foundation that shape your experiences. If you believe that your worth comes from being endlessly accommodating, you'll struggle to say no. When you shift your internal narrative, you change what and who you attract.

- Sometimes, success doesn't feel hard because it's hard—it feels hard because it separates us. For women who've been conditioned to maintain harmony, that separation feels like a wound we're not supposed to cause. But rising isn't abandonment. There is no need to apologize for leveling up. Don't shrink to make others comfortable. Step up and don't look back.

FOURTEEN

GROW INTO WHO YOU ALREADY ARE

SO MUCH OF WHAT HOLDS US BACK ISN'T ABOUT what's happening *outside* of us—it's what's going on *inside*. Cultural messages and past experiences shape us, but in my work, I've found that most of the time, it's internal hesitation, guilt, or fear that creates the biggest roadblocks.

This is where a mentor becomes so important. When you're in the thick of it, emotion clouds reason.

Too often, especially among women, we anticipate envy or discomfort when we grow. We brace for resentment when we should be celebrating. Women are not always taught to cheer each other on when someone steps forward into something bigger. Instead, we can become anxious about being "too much," or making someone else feel "less than." We twist ourselves in knots to avoid disrupting the emotional equilibrium of others, but that's not healthy. It's not how we build a community of empowered, aligned women.

Let's do better for each other. Let's be the friend who says, "I'm so proud of you." Let's stop resenting each other's wins and start learning from them. We all rise higher when we refuse to compete from a place of insecurity and instead celebrate from a place of confidence.

For those of us who are mentors, or who have the honor of guiding others in this journey, let's remember the power of clarity. Sometimes, just breaking something down step by step can be the lifeline someone needs to step into their next chapter with courage.

Boundaries Begin with Identity

When women step fully into their professional identity, boundaries become possible—sometimes for the very first time. We often talk about boundaries like they're tools you learn to wield, but in my experience, they stem more from how you see yourself than from what you know. When you *believe* you're a professional, you give yourself permission to behave like one. That includes saying no, taking time off, and expecting to be compensated fairly.

So many women in the equestrian world, particularly younger professionals, struggle to create and maintain reasonable boundaries. I recently worked with a thirty-something trainer who was agonizing over how to tell her clients she was going on vacation. A *vacation*. This was not a sabbatical or a disappearance, just a short, well-deserved break after months of nonstop service. Still, the guilt she carried was immense.

She was afraid her clients would be upset, or that they might even leave. Underneath all that fear was a core belief that her job was to keep everyone happy all the time.

So I asked her, "What is your job as a professional? Your job is to care for the horses, to keep them sound and happy, to support your clients with integrity and expertise. It does *not* mean abandoning your own well-being to meet every whim."

For women, boundaries often feel like betrayals. We've been conditioned to be nice, to be agreeable, to be helpful, and while those qualities aren't inherently bad, they become dangerous when they override our ability to take care of ourselves.

That's why stepping into a solid identity is so powerful. When you identify as a capable, experienced professional, it becomes easier to say things like:

- "I am raising my rates."
- "I'm not available for lessons after 6 p.m."
- "I'll be out of town next week. I have coverage arranged, but I will be on vacation."

These are not outrageous demands. They are standard, reasonable boundaries that any client (any client worth keeping, at least) will understand and respect.

This is another area where mentorship becomes so critical. What may seem obvious to a mentor isn't always obvious when you're in the thick of it. It's not obvious when you're exhausted and worried and trying to do right by everyone. That's why it matters to have someone more experienced who can say, "Here's what to say. Here's how to say it. And here's why you're *absolutely* allowed to."

In my work as a performance psychologist and mentor, I often feel like a mirror reflecting back to my clients what they already know but can't quite believe. I'm giving language to boundaries they've been too afraid to speak.

Sometimes all it takes is a shift in identity from the people-pleasing caretaker to the skilled professional. From someone who's constantly apologizing for her needs to someone who understands her worth.

This is not selfish. It's the first step toward building a sustainable, fulfilling career in a world that too often asks us to give more than we can afford.

Setting the Tone for Your Life

I remember a friend telling me about watching two very different documentaries in the same week. One featured Britney Spears, showing the heartbreaking consequences of surrendering control and allowing others to dictate her life. The other was about Pink, who exuded a fierce sense of ownership over her choices, career, and body. It struck my friend how clearly identity influenced their trajectories. One woman believed herself to be powerful and lived like it. The other had her power stripped from her, and for a long time, didn't push back.

Identity matters. It sets the tone for everything we think, feel, and do.

We are often handed identities: mother, helper, good girl, people pleaser. But the true work is reclaiming the right to define ourselves *on purpose.*

For me, as I said, that reckoning came during the years I spent focused entirely on motherhood. At some point, I knew something was missing. For a time, I explored interior design. People had often complimented my style, and I helped friends decorate their homes. I enrolled in classes and took on some small jobs, but something still felt off. I didn't like being told what kind of room to create, or the constant churn of trends and consumerism.

Most of all, I realized what I loved wasn't the furniture but *the people.* What I really enjoyed was asking, "Who are you? What do we need to change in your space for it to bring you joy?" That's when I knew it was the *psychological* part I was drawn to all along. So I came back home to what I knew I was meant to do. I am a psychologist. That's where I find the most fulfillment.

When women suppress this process of intentional rediscovery, they suffer. I've seen it in my clients, especially those who deny or dilute who they truly are out of guilt, fear, or obligation. A good example is the trainer who kept poor-fit clients far too long. When she finally stepped up into a new training arrangement that aligned with her sense of self and ambition, everything changed. Not just the logistics of her business, but her *happiness.*

When you live out of sync with who you are, no amount of external validation will fill the gap. But when you step into the fullness of who you're meant to be, you create the conditions for real, lasting contentment.

You don't have to know your path perfectly. You can experiment and try on identities. Say no when something doesn't fit, but keep coming back to the deeper question: *Does this feel like me?* And then, be intentional in what you choose to claim.

Afraid to Say It

Sometimes, we as women know exactly what we want, but we are afraid to say it out loud. Or we say it in a whisper, a half joke, a throwaway line we don't expect anyone to take seriously.

I think of the talented rider who once admitted to me, almost sheepishly, that her goal was "world domination." She laughed nervously after saying it, immediately shrinking back from her own words. It wasn't something she'd dare say to anyone else, but she trusted me. I knew she was being honest. That was her truth. The problem wasn't the dream. It was the disconnect between that big vision and how she was showing up around other people in her daily life.

There's a term for this: *identity discrepancy*. When an athlete's current self-image doesn't match her aspirations, there's conflict. Maybe she keeps her goals tucked away in private, telling herself she's not ready, not good enough, or that she might make others uncomfortable by aiming too high. That tension can stall progress, or worse, cause a slow, quiet erosion of self-belief.

When I work with clients, my job isn't to force anyone forward. It's to see them, to notice the gap between how they talk and what they actually want, and then speak to the disconnect. Most importantly, I help them *hold the vision.*

I hold the vision when they're afraid of it. I hold it when they feel unworthy of it. I hold it when it's easier for them to play small. One client told me, "You're my accountability. You keep me honest with myself." She wasn't talking about to-do lists or calendars. She meant I helped her remember who she really was, even when she forgot.

This is about creating a space that is safe enough and big enough for women to grow into who they already are. Sometimes, that starts with asking them a few simple questions.

If you don't have a mentor, you can do this for yourself. Ask the following questions:

- Is how I'm showing up in the world aligned with what I really want?
- Am I shrinking myself to fit others' expectations?
- Do I allow myself to dream big, or do I apologize for my ambitions?

- Is there a part of me I've buried because it feels like "too much"?
- Who do I need to become to claim the goals I secretly hold?

You don't need to have perfect answers. You don't even need to say your dreams out loud yet, but begin noticing the gap. When your identity starts to match your aspirations, your world begins to change for the better. You start to ride differently, lead differently, and *live* differently.

In the next section, we'll begin exploring how to close that gap—how to step into the woman you're becoming. But for now, give yourself the gift of honesty. What's the dream? And are you willing to believe it belongs to you?

KEY TAKEAWAYS

- When women step fully into their professional identities, boundaries become possible—sometimes for the very first time. We often talk about boundaries like they're tools you learn to wield, but in my experience, they stem more from how you see yourself than from what you know. One example: When you identify as a professional, you give yourself permission to think, act, and lead like one. That includes saying no, taking time off, and expecting to be compensated fairly.

- When you live out of sync with who you are, no amount of external validation will fill the gap. But when you step into the fullness of who you're meant to be, you create the conditions for real, lasting contentment.

PART III

BUILDING YOUR TRAIL MAP

FIFTEEN

WHERE DO YOU WANT TO BE?

MANY OF THE PEOPLE I WORK WITH COME TO me overwhelmed. They're frustrated with clients, burned out by logistics, or tangled up in the daily grind of running their business. They bring me the mess, but what I see is not failure. More than anything, I see a lack of alignment.

I invite them to fly up to ten thousand feet with me to take a big-picture look at their lives. I say, "We can't begin moving forward until we know where we're going. Let's find your destination and set your compass."

That's when I ask one of my favorite questions: *Where do you want to be in ten years?*

I mean it. I'm not asking for a reasonable projection. I'm asking them to step out of the tangle of today's stress and doubt and into the possibility of their future. Often, they start with a glimmer of a dream, and then immediately follow it with all the reasons it won't happen.

"Well, I'd love to do that, but it's not realistic. We don't have the money. My clients wouldn't go for it. I'm not ready."

When that happens, I stop them. "Those aren't the rules right now," I say. "This part is playful. This is dream time. You're not buying anything yet—we're just trying it on."

I liken it to a trip to a fancy department store. You walk through the store and grab whatever catches your eye, even the expensive pieces and the bold colors. You take them into the fitting room and try them on—not to commit, but to see what fits, what flatters, what *feels* right. It's the same with your life. You try on a future to see how it moves on you.

So we play: *What does your business look like in ten years? Where do you live? Who's with you? How do your days look and feel?*

Once we've stretched that long-term vision muscle, we start to zoom back in. *What would five years out look like if that ten-year vision were true? What about two and a half years? One year?*

Slowly, we build a bridge from the imagined future back to today. Once you know where you're going, your choices start to change. Every decision, big or small, is determined by the vision.

I often put it like this: If you want to become the Ritz-Carlton of your world, you have to start making Ritz-Carlton decisions. Everything about the Ritz-Carlton is five-star, from start to finish. You don't become the best by accident. You show up that way, in small ways and large—starting right now.

So what does a "Ritz-Carlton version" of you look like right now? Maybe it's setting better boundaries. Maybe it's raising your rates. Maybe it's walking into the barn or office with a little more clarity, confidence, and calm. Maybe it means showing up on time and well-prepared, with care, clarity, and excellence.

It's not about just big decisions. It's the little ones too. You dress the part. You speak the part. You honor your own time and energy the way you would expect a top-tier professional to do. When you do that, other people start treating you that way too.

In contrast, if you show up like a budget motel, then that's the energy you invite back. People will undervalue you if you undervalue yourself. I always say that at the Ritz-Carlton, they don't give you the cheap little soaps in the bathroom. You get top quality across the board, from the soaps to the linens, because that is the Ritz-Carlton standard.

All too often, I find professionals hiring staff that don't align with the mission. I also see professionals who endure clients who don't treat them well, not to mention undercharging, over-giving, and trying to be everything to everyone while slowly burning out. It doesn't work, but they do it because their identity is not aligned with their vision, or they haven't fully allowed themselves to embrace their vision.

Once you're clear on who you want to become, then you can begin to *intentionally* choose the actions that align with that version of you.

Intentionality is powerful.

So for now, as a simple step, start with that one question:

1. What does my life look like in ten years?

Not what you *think* it should look like. Not what your parents or your clients or your trainer expect it to look like. What do *you* want it to look like? Try it on. Don't overthink it. Just dream a little. Get playful, and as you hold that vision, ask yourself this too:

2. Who are the people I need around me to help me get there?

No matter how strong your vision is, you can't build it alone. You need to be surrounded by people who see you—not just support you, but *really* see you. That's part of my role with the women I work with. I hold the vision with them, even when they forget, even when they get scared, even when the world tries to shrink them back into someone smaller.

If you don't yet have those people in your corner, go find them. Seek out mentors, friends, and peers who lift you up, who challenge you, who say, "I see you, and I believe in where you're going." You deserve nothing less.

Not Everyone Will Come with You

As you begin to step into a fuller version of yourself—whether that means taking on a new professional role, setting firmer boundaries, or pursuing a dream that feels big and bold—it's important to recognize that not everyone in your life will come with you. And that's okay.

Some people will support you with their whole hearts. Others will hesitate, and a few may actively resist your growth because they're afraid or envious.

Fear is often disguised as concern. It shows up in the form of "helpful" advice or subtle discouragement: "Are you sure that's practical? Maybe you should stick with something more stable. Is there really a market for that?"

What they're really saying is "I don't understand this path, and it scares me."

That young client of mine who comes from an affluent family has had to deal with this type of discouragement. She has a loving, well-meaning family, but they don't grasp her vision. She wanted to create a life in the horse industry, blending her training business with social media and marketing work. It was a creative, multidimensional dream that didn't follow a traditional path. Her parents, out of their own fears, urged her to find a more "stable" job, but that wouldn't fulfill her.

They weren't trying to hurt her. They simply didn't know how to support a dream that looked different from the one they had envisioned.

Bear in mind, the bolder your vision, the more it may trigger other people's insecurities or competitiveness, especially if your identity begins to shift in ways that make them uncomfortable. That's why resilience is so important.

When someone you care about reacts negatively to your growth, it can be painful. It's tempting to defer your dream for the sake of keeping the peace, but you must remember who you are and where you're going.

The disappointment of not being supported must never outweigh your responsibility to live in alignment with your truth.

During a dinner conversation with one of my old mentors, I shared that I was writing this book—a project that I have mulled over for a long while and care deeply about. His off-the-cuff response was, "Is there really a need for that?" He meant no harm, but it stung. I carried that comment with me for far longer than I'd like to admit. It echoed in moments of doubt, and it's why I'm so passionate about helping others hold firm when those moments come. Because they *will* come.

This is exactly why the people around you matter so much. You need to gather a circle of supporters who truly believe in your potential, who reflect your vision back to you, especially on days when you forget it yourself.

That identity shift is not always easy. It's hard-won and hard-fought, and it's often challenged. But it's worth it. When you finally claim that identity, you become unstoppable. You begin to attract people, opportunities, and experiences that align with who you really are, and you no longer need to seek permission from others to live a life that lights you up.

KEY TAKEAWAYS

- If you feel overwhelmed—frustrated with clients, burned out by logistics, or tangled up in the daily grind of running your business—chances are it's a lack of alignment. I invite you to fly up to ten thousand feet and take a big-picture look at your life. To do that, start by considering the questions: *Where do you want to be in ten years? What does your business look like in ten years? Where do you live? Who's with you? How do your days look and feel?*

- Once you've stretched that long-term vision muscle, start to zoom back in. *What would five years out look like if that ten-year vision were true? What about two and a half years? One year?* The idea is to build a bridge from the imagined future back to today.

- Once you're clear on who you want to become, then you can begin to intentionally choose the thoughts and actions that align with that version of you.

SIXTEEN

STEPPING INTO A BIGGER LIFE

WHEN I BEGIN WORKING WITH A NEW CLIENT, or even just having an initial conversation, I pay close attention to the energy they're bringing. That might sound a little abstract, but it's an important part of the process of healing. To do meaningful work, I need to understand the frequency at which they're operating: their mindset, emotional state, and sense of purpose.

I have to meet people where they are, but if we're aiming to create something bigger, we have to help them reach a higher frequency. That elevated frequency is rooted in purpose. It's about doing more than simply accumulating clients or chasing surface-level success, but living in alignment and contributing something meaningful to the world. When a woman is tuned into her deeper purpose, it's unmistakable. You can feel it, and when she's not, that dissonance is just as evident.

Whether it's in the saddle or sitting at your desk, some days you just know you feel off. You're scattered, or you're doubting yourself. Those are the moments that require recalibration and a return to intention. I catch myself in this space too, whether I'm writing an article or schooling one of my horses. I'll realize I'm ungrounded, not fully present, and I have to reset. That's part of the regular work.

When something isn't quite right, you know it. You feel it in your gut. Whether it's a client relationship, a training ride, or even a paragraph you've written, the disharmony is unmistakable. Fortunately, once you tune in, it's also easy to spot and easy to adjust. You just bring it back into alignment with your deeper purpose.

That's why I always encourage my clients to be intentional in their choices but also in the energy they bring to everything they do. Your resonance is your calling card. Remember, if you want to work at an elite level, you have to show up that way. Every interaction and every small decision matters because the way you show up is the way the world treats you.

This morning, for example, I put on my red lipstick. I certainly didn't *need* red lipstick, but it made me feel vibrant. It helped me show up with the energy I wanted to bring, which in turn helped me step into something meaningful. This is just a small example of how we make intentional choices to elevate the energy we bring to a situation. And the energy you bring is just as important as the work you do.

The fact is, powerful women know how to step into their own power. But not just that: They create other powerful women. That's what my work is about. The most powerful women I know are not those who hoard knowledge, status, or attention. They are the ones who lift others up. They see the potential in another woman and say, "Come on, let's go. You belong here too."

Unfortunately, not everyone is wired that way. I'm working right now with a woman who's been in a difficult professional relationship for years. She works with a world-class rider, but instead of lifting her up, this rider hoards power and attention. She's driven by insecurity, and my client, though a thoughtful and talented assistant, has remained in the shadows far too long.

My client is ready for something more, but she's risk-averse. She has spent years being made to feel small, and that conditioning doesn't disappear overnight. In reality, she has outgrown her current role, and she's beginning to see that it's not going to change.

That's the shift I'm after: that moment when a woman realizes she no longer has to ask permission to be powerful. It starts with your resonance, your energy, and it continues with a willingness to let go of relationships or roles that dim your light instead of reflecting it.

So, right now, ask yourself: *Am I resonating at the frequency of the life I want to live? Am I surrounding myself with people who lift me, challenge me, and truly see me?*

If the answer is no, that means it's time to adjust. The right people, the right energy, and the right opportunities are all out there, but first, you have to rise to meet them.

Put Your Red Lipstick On

Sometimes, the turning point in a client's life is as simple as one moment of clarity and courage. That client who is working with the high-profile professional? She recently found herself at a crossroads: An accomplished businesswoman was interested in hiring her. This woman runs a major company, thinks expansively, and moves boldly. My client had a chance to join forces with her, but this powerful woman operated at a high frequency. My client could feel the potential, but she also felt unsure. Could she rise to meet it?

As we talked near the end of our session, I didn't have time to unpack it all with her, but I knew what needed to be said. I stopped her and said, "Put your red lipstick on." Now, I know this young woman would *never* actually wear red lipstick. I used the line as a metaphor to convey my message: "Put on your red lipstick. Show up bigger. Walk into that meeting with the confidence you haven't yet claimed."

I reminded her that the woman who was offering the opportunity *expects* boldness. She thinks big; she's not likely to blink when my client asks for a real salary and benefits. In fact, she probably expects it. But my client was still thinking in the shadow of her old environment: small, hesitant, unsure.

I told her, "You've got to think big. You're stepping into a conversation with someone who has a big vision and wants to collaborate, not dominate. What could you build together? What are your dreams? Speak them out loud. I promise she'll meet you there."

Remember, vision and intention are powerful. If we can think it, and then say it, we can start to create it.

A similar situation arose with another client—a professional in her early thirties who runs a training program and riding school. She's talented and driven, but for years, she struggled to claim her place at the next level. She made common mistakes: undercharging, overworking, hiring the wrong help, tolerating clients who didn't align with her goals. Her decisions came from a place of fear and scarcity, not from the vision of who she truly was and where she wanted to go.

Nine months ago, she lost a couple of clients in her training program. Panicked, she was ready to fill the stalls with anyone who walked down the street with a horse. I stopped her. "No. I won't let you do that. You don't get to panic-fill your barn. You're building something bigger."

Together, we zoomed out. "Where are we going?" I asked her. "What do you want your program to become?" When we focused on the long-term vision, the answer to who belonged in those stalls became clear.

Soon after, a client of hers announced she wanted to take a trip to Europe to buy several high-end horses. She and my client flew overseas, and they returned with two world-class horses. Guess who is now occupying those two stalls!

But then the next challenge emerged: identity. My client suddenly found herself standing in the middle of what she'd always dreamed of, and she was overwhelmed. "Do I belong here?" she wondered. "Can I do this?"

And my job was to remind her: *This is what you were aiming for.*

The moment we begin to think bigger, to speak our worth, and to surround ourselves with others who operate at that higher level, everything changes. So the next time you're walking into a conversation, a negotiation, or a new chapter, *put your metaphorical (and possibly literal) red lipstick on.* Yes, this is part of your trail map. After all, you're not just stepping into a role. You're stepping into *you.*

Lead Like the Professional You're Becoming

Recently, one of my longtime clients hit a familiar snag. On paper, she's thriving. There are twenty-six horses in her dressage program, and she has new high-level clients bringing in new Grand Prix prospects. Despite the upward trajectory of her career, though, I could see warning signs—she was starting to think small.

She was cobbling together a support team that didn't match the caliber of her vision. One assistant was reliable but didn't have a dressage background. Another was a college student—well-meaning but inconsistent. It was patchwork, and entirely out of sync with the destination.

So I asked her, "Where are we going? Because if we're talking about World Cup–level horses, then everything needs to be at that level: the standards, the systems, the self-image. You can't train at the top of the sport and staff your barn like it's a B-level program. You can't keep looking down at the dirt and expect to soar. Lift your eyes. Stop staring at the problems at your feet. Where are we going?"

Once you know the destination, the rest becomes clear. If you're aiming for international competition, *everything* has to align with that vision. That means assistants who are trained and trustworthy. That means systems that run with clarity and precision. That means boundaries with clients. And it means *you*, the leader, showing up and carrying yourself like the professional you already are.

We walked through it together. "Let's imagine this is five years down the road. What does your business look like? If the goal is to manage multiple international horses, then it's not just about this one client anymore. It's about building a program for three or four clients at that elite level. That is who you are now."

What's happening in her world is exciting. She's never had this many upper-level horses. She's never operated at this level, and she has to fight the urge to shrink, to scatter, to feel guilty for having new expectations and setting new boundaries.

Just like this client, an integral part of your trail map is learning to carry yourself like a leader, not like someone still apologizing for having to hold a boundary. That isn't arrogance. It's alignment.

Remember, you have to look where you want to go, because you'll go where you look.

If you keep looking down at the mess, you'll keep building small. If you look up and out, toward the vision, you'll start building what you're truly meant for.

So much of what we carry into the arena starts with how we show up. I'm not just talking about your mindset, but also how you dress, speak, and carry yourself. That's why one of the most important things I remind my clients is this: *Look the part. Live the part. Be proud of who you're becoming, even before you fully arrive.*

What we think is what we create.

Even women who've been working with me for years, growing and making progress, still find themselves slipping back into old habits. They get stuck in the muck, looking down, thinking small, dressing like they don't belong, or apologizing for taking up space.

One of my clients recently admitted she'd been riding in six-dollar tank tops and worn-out breeches because she thought, *Well, I'm not riding at the top levels, so why bother?* But when she finally bought a new outfit that reflected her dedication to her horse and her sport, it changed the way she rode. She felt proud and confident, and that energy carried through to her horse and the whole experience.

Yet again, I encourage you: Wear the red lipstick. It's a symbol, a reminder that you belong in the ring, and it's time to show up like it.

KEY TAKEAWAYS

- As you do this work, be intentional in the energy you bring to everything you do. Your resonance is your calling card. Every interaction and every decision matters, because how you show up is what you attract.

- When something isn't quite right, you know it. You feel it in your gut. Whether it's a client relationship, a training ride, or even a paragraph you've written, the disharmony is unmistakable. Fortunately, once you tune in, it's also easy to spot and easy to adjust. You just bring it back into alignment with your deeper purpose.

- Right now, ask yourself: *Am I resonating at the frequency of the life I want to live? Am I surrounding myself with people who lift me, challenge me, and truly see me?* If the answer is no, that means it's time to adjust. The right people, the right energy, and the right opportunities are all out there, but first, you have to rise to meet them.

- What you think is what you create.

SEVENTEEN

ALLOW YOURSELF TO SHINE

YEARS AGO, I HAD A CONVERSATION WITH A coach—someone I thought might be able to support me on my journey as I stepped more fully into the work of sports and performance coaching. I also thought she might help me elevate my own riding. We were in the middle of a fairly standard introductory conversation when, seemingly out of nowhere, she said to me, "Wait, so you want to do what I do? *You want me to help you compete with me?*" She seemed shocked.

I was taken aback. It wasn't just that she was being rude or defensive—it was that her whole frame of reference was so small, so fear-driven, that she saw another woman's growth and request for help as a threat. She saw my potential not as something to be encouraged, but as something to guard against.

I gathered myself and replied, "Actually, yes. As a psychologist, one of the foundational principles of our work is teaching others. I've spent many years training and mentoring other psychologists. It's part of our responsibility as professionals."

Think about it: In medicine, new doctors are mentored and trained by experienced physicians. It's how skills and wisdom get passed down. No one says, "Sorry, I'm not going to teach you how to perform this surgery. You might do it better than me someday." That would be absurd.

The same should hold true in coaching, in horsemanship, in leadership—anywhere. But this woman didn't see it that way. She was too busy protecting her turf. At some point she told me to get certified through the Tony Robbins program, which seemed to me a shocking disregard of my extensive training and experience. I ended the call politely but firmly, knowing immediately that this was someone I'd never collaborate with.

She was operating from a scarcity mindset. A mindset that says, "The pie is small, and if you win, I lose." That kind of thinking has no place in the world I'm building. In fact, my experience is that powerful people lift others up. Confident horsewomen create more confident horsewomen. Powerful female entrepreneurs create more powerful female entrepreneurs.

At its heart, this lesson is simple: Real leaders don't fear competition—they welcome it, they support it, they cheer it on. They understand that when you lead from a place of abundance, collaboration, and confidence, the right people show up and the right opportunities appear. The fear-based voices fade into the background where they belong.

From Competition to Community

There's something truly powerful in embracing the idea that *there is enough*—enough opportunity, enough community, enough room for all of us to rise. A rising tide really *does* lift all boats.

It's a concept I repeatedly emphasize in my work.

> **While we may be in competition with each other, we are also in community with each other. When we surround ourselves with women who are powerful, skilled, and passionate, we don't shrink. We rise.**

High-quality competition spurs high-quality performance.

I get better when I'm around people who are better. When I compete against great riders, I am lifted up. That's where the growth happens. And yet, this fear of not being "enough" shows up all the time, especially with women who are still finding their footing.

One of my clients, a trainer five years into her career, was preparing to take a student to a high-profile show in Kentucky. She confessed to me that she felt intimidated standing beside big names like John French and Scott Stewart.

She said, "I just don't feel like I belong there."

You probably already know what I'm going to say. After all, no one expects her to be someone she's not. She's *not* Scott Stewart, and that's okay. There's no shame in being exactly where she is, and I'm certainly not going to let her shrink herself because of it. Remember: Even those top professionals started at the beginning.

So I told her, "Go to that show. Stand tall. Coach your rider with confidence. Then absorb everything around you. Watch the greats. Listen to what they say. Learn. That's the kind of fearlessness we're after. It's not ego, but a deep-rooted willingness to grow."

You don't grow by hiding. You grow by showing up. That old saying is exactly right: *If you're the smartest person in the room, you're in the wrong room.* Growth requires challenge. Expansion requires exposure. And yes, sometimes it's uncomfortable, but that's where transformation happens.

So when clients ask me, "Where do I even start?" I tell them, "All you have to do is start. All roads lead to Rome. Start where you are, and we'll get where you need to go. You don't need to have it all figured out. And if at any point you feel yourself shrinking, getting mired in the muck, or stuck in comparison, pause and look up. Put on the metaphorical red lipstick. Wear the breeches that make you feel strong. Straighten your spine, lift your energy, and remember that you belong here."

I live this truth in my own practice every day. People sometimes ask me, "How do you begin work with a new client?" The honest answer is I don't follow a rigid structure. I don't believe in traditional intake interviews. That approach can shut people down or steer them away from their real truth. Instead, I start where they are.

When someone comes to me, they bring exactly what I need to know. I simply ask, "Tell me what's going on," and from there, they hand me the map. I might ask for more context, just enough to understand their world, but I trust that people know, deep down, where the work needs to begin.

That's what I mean when I say, "All roads lead to Rome." Wherever we start, we will eventually arrive where we need to be.

Let Yourself Glow

Earlier this week, I had a first session with a new client. She's a real estate professional, newly engaged, and a serious equestrian. She's high-energy; her brain fires fast, and she talks at one hundred miles per hour. From the moment we started, I could feel the intensity humming beneath the surface.

She came to me because she recently had a scary accident where her horse slipped and fell, and she was injured. Now she's back in the saddle but haunted by fear. That's a common entry point for working with a new client.

She mentioned she was going to a show soon and was fixated on the idea that the accident would happen again. She was replaying the past as if it were guaranteed to repeat, so we worked through that. I helped her learn how to stay present and ride every step in real time instead of reacting to ghosts.

However, as we talked, something deeper began to surface. As we explored more, I began asking questions about her work. Was this pattern of anticipating failure—this fear-based thinking—showing up there too?

"Absolutely," she replied. She admitted to being a perfectionist. One mistake, and she would unravel emotionally.

This wasn't just about riding. This was a woman who was highly competitive and deeply driven, and what she was *really* afraid of wasn't just another fall—it was how big her dreams truly were. Eventually, those dreams came out: She didn't just want to ride again. She wanted to compete in eventing *at the highest level.*

That revelation hit like a lightning bolt. Her fear of falling was real, yes, but it was also camouflage. Beneath it was the terror of stepping fully into her potential.

She had just come off a show the previous weekend where she performed beautifully. She started off tentatively, but by the end, she was confident and composed. She even placed third, but more importantly, she grew emotionally and athletically. It was a win on every level, yet she couldn't acknowledge it, much less savor it.

The moment the show ended, she leapt forward in her mind to the next one. "What if I move up a level and blow it? What if it all goes wrong?"

So I asked her: "When you close a big real estate deal, do you let yourself glow a little? Do you shine brighter afterward?"

"Oh, absolutely," she said without hesitation.

"Then why not here?" I pressed. "Why can't you hold this success a little longer? You're already casting doubt on what's next before you've let yourself *own* the win."

It was a breakthrough moment. This was someone who knew how to celebrate herself in one arena but had never learned to do it in another.

So I gave her an assignment: *Hold on to all the wins from the show—not just the ribbon, but the real accomplishments: the trust, the focus, the composure, the courage. Let them feed your confidence.*

I invite you, as you walk the path to claiming your power, to do the same. Embrace the courage that's inside of you—the courage that allows you to peel back the layers and see what's really going on beneath the fear. Because most of the time, what's underneath isn't weakness at all—it's your power, waiting to be claimed.

Embody Your Presence

Recently, I started working with a competitive rider who had just returned from a show. She had performed incredibly well, both technically and mentally. She'd made a mistake in one round where she added in an extra stride at a fence, but overall, she was successful on many levels. The problem is that she couldn't stop obsessing over that one mistake, replaying it again and again and beating herself up.

So I stopped her and asked her to tell me everything she was proud of—every technical choice that worked, every moment she stayed composed, every time she supported herself mentally instead of spiraling. That became her assignment for the week: to savor all of those things. No further dissection of what went wrong, no fast-forwarding to disaster scenarios about the next show. Just staying present with the feeling of pride.

"You may be tempted to go back to that critical voice," I told her. "But when you catch yourself doing that, I want you to redirect. Practice savoring, just like you do at work when you solve a tough problem."

This client has *big* dreams. Sometimes, that kind of drive can feel frightening, so the mind grabs onto what seems like a "safer" fear to disguise the much deeper vulnerability: the fear of playing big.

As we kept talking, it became clear that her intensity and competitiveness were part of what was driving her, but she hadn't made peace with those qualities yet. Instead of lifting her up, her ambition was dragging her down. So now, part of our work is to help her befriend her competitiveness, to channel it as a strength, not let it become a weight.

This is work that I do with many of my clients, and it's work I invite you to start doing too. It starts with recognizing that you're not just correcting a mindset; you're *relating differently* to who you are. I want my client to learn to be proud of her ambition, not ashamed of it. I want her to understand that being driven doesn't

make her "too much." It makes her powerful, but only if she's willing to own it.

Most of us bring similar internal patterns into every arena of life. If you're a perfectionist in the saddle, there's a good chance you carry that same energy into your relationships, your work, your parenting. You might express it differently depending on the environment, but your way of thinking and feeling follows you wherever you go.

That's why I often ask my clients, "Where else in your life do you see this pattern showing up?" Sometimes the answers surprise them. One rider I worked with owned a tech company and was also a mother of teenage boys. I watched how clear and confident she was with her sons—setting boundaries, giving direction, holding space. But in her professional life, that clarity disappeared. She didn't hold her staff accountable, and she second-guessed herself constantly.

I helped her connect those two identities. I said, "The woman who's such a great mom? She can also lead a team. She can also run a business." Once she saw that consistency of character, things began to change. She started to embody that same confident presence at work.

I invite my clients—and now you—to do some self-assessment. Where in your life do you feel strong, proud, capable? Where do you consistently show up with clarity and confidence? And where do you feel small, hesitant, or unsure?

Chances are, you're more consistent than you think, but if you notice discrepancies between parts of your life, be curious about them. Don't judge—observe. That curiosity can open up powerful new possibilities for growth and alignment.

As you reflect, remember, no part of your life is separate from the others. The same inner qualities that make you powerful in one area can serve you in others too. And when you start to integrate those strengths across all parts of yourself, you'll be well on your way to living from a place of deep, sustainable confidence.

KEY TAKEAWAYS

- Real leaders don't fear competition—they welcome it, they support it, they seek it out. They understand that when you lead from a place of abundance, collaboration, and confidence, the right people show up and the right opportunities appear. The fear-based voices fade into the background where they belong.

- There's something truly powerful in embracing the idea that there is enough—enough opportunity, enough community, enough room for all of us to rise. A rising tide really does lift all boats.

- We may technically be in competition with each other, but more importantly, we're also in community with each other. When we surround ourselves with women who are powerful, skilled, and passionate, we don't shrink. We rise.

- If you're wondering where to start, *start at the beginning*. All roads lead to Rome. Start where you are, and we'll get where you need to go. You don't need to have it all figured out. And if at any point you feel yourself shrinking, getting mired in the muck, or stuck in comparison, pause and look up. Straighten your spine, lift your energy, and remember that you belong here.

EIGHTEEN

FIND YOUR WHY

YOUR *WHY* IS YOUR FOUNDATION—YOUR NORTH Star. Without it, the whole structure of your pursuit wobbles, yet it's astonishing how many of my clients lose their *why* along the way. For a lot of them—many of whom are top equestrians—that's a big problem. This sport is financially, physically, and emotionally challenging. It's not for the faint of heart. If you don't know *why* you're doing it, if you're not anchored in some deeper meaning, burnout becomes almost inevitable.

That's why I always ask clients, "Why are you riding? Why do you show up? What does this mean to you?"

There's no one right answer. It might be the bond with your horse, or the joy of progress, or maybe the thrill of competition.

You might like the way it quiets your mind or reconnects you with your strength. What matters is that *you* know the answer, and that you keep coming back to it.

One of my clients just turned down a substantial lease offer on one of her geldings. It was a tempting sum, especially after the horse had come back from an injury and was once again performing beautifully. On paper, it seemed like a no-brainer, but she ultimately turned it down. Then she came to me, full of doubt.

"Did I make a stupid financial decision?" she asked. "Was that just foolish sentimentality?"

I looked at her and asked, "Do you love this horse?"

Her answer, unequivocally, was yes.

That horse wasn't just an asset. He was a partner and a teammate, a source of confidence and joy. We went back to her *why* and explored what mattered most to her in this relationship and in the sport. From there, the answer became clear—she had made the right choice for her.

Whether you ride or not, there's a deeply valuable lesson here:

> **Your *why* isn't about pleasing others—whether that's your father, your husband, your trainer, or society at large—and it's not about what's logical on paper. It's about what anchors you and sustains you when the inevitable challenges arise.**

Once you're clear on your *why*, the next step is clarifying where you want to go. What's the vision? What does success look like? From that clarity, everything else flows. Decisions become easier. Mistakes lose their sting. Progress feels more meaningful. You begin to process your experiences less like a critic and more like a compassionate guide to yourself.

In my seminars, we often move from *why* to a personal mission statement. Your mission statement is a distillation of what you're about, not just what you do but how you *think* about what you do. How you walk into the barn. How you respond to fear. How you treat your horse. Your mission is your ethos, and once it's clear, it shapes everything from how you train, to how you show, to how you come back from a fall. Your mission is how your *why* plays out in the real world. It's the fusion of intention and action. It's your compass for how you train, how you compete, and how you carry yourself, both in and out of the ring.

Get Clear on Your Why

When it comes to identifying your *why*, the more specific you can be, the better. Furthermore, I recommend cultivating more than one *why*. You'll likely have a core *why* for your riding life, a different one for your professional life, and perhaps even one for your role as a parent, partner, or friend. These *why* statements clarify your decisions, especially when things get tough or confusing. They bring meaning to the hard work and the setbacks, not just the blue ribbons.

Maybe today, your *why* is: *I want to show up as the best version of myself and help my horse do the same.* Or maybe, across your life as a rider, your *why* is: *To cultivate excellence in myself and partnership with my horse, regardless of outcome.* Either way, when your intention is clear, the purpose of every ride is also clear.

Your *why* helps reframe competition too. When you're aligned with your own *why*, you stop measuring your success by someone else's result. You stop shrinking in comparison to someone whose horse might have better breeding or more expressive movement. You stop silently celebrating if their horse misses a flying change because it bumps you up the placings. That kind of comparison-based, scarcity-driven competition only makes you smaller. It pulls you down energetically, and ultimately, it steals your joy.

Instead, when your *why* is centered on showing up fully and helping your horse show up fully, you celebrate when you do your job well. You are proud when your horse tries his heart out, and you can be genuinely happy when your competitor nails her changes too, because her success doesn't take anything away from you. In fact, it lifts you up.

The paradox of real excellence is that it's expansive, not competitive in the traditional sense. You can still strive. You can still be ambitious. You can still want to win. But your *why* keeps you grounded. Your *why* protects you from the bitterness, envy, and self-doubt that can creep in when your focus drifts outside yourself, and it makes the journey infinitely more joyful.

Let your *why* be the thread that ties everything together: your ambition, your relationship with your horse, your decisions, and your self-talk. It's not a luxury but a necessity, and if you let it anchor you, it will serve you again and again.

KEY TAKEAWAYS

- Your *why* isn't about pleasing others, and it's not about what's logical on paper. It's about what anchors you and sustains you when the inevitable challenges arise.

- Once you're clear on your *why*, the next step is clarifying where you want to go. What's the vision? What does success look like? From that clarity, everything else flows. Decisions become easier. Mistakes lose their sting. Progress feels more meaningful. You begin to process your experiences less like a critic, and more like a compassionate guide to yourself.

- It's often helpful to move from *why* to a personal mission statement. Your mission statement is a distillation of what you're about, not just what you do but how you think about what you do. How you walk through life. How you respond to fear. How you treat the people around you. Your mission is your ethos, and once it's clear, it begins to shape everything—your mindset, your feelings, and your choices.

- When your *why* is centered on showing up fully, you can be proud when you do your job well. You can be genuinely happy when other women succeed too, because their success doesn't take anything away from you. In fact, it lifts you up. That's the paradox of real excellence. It's expansive, not competitive in the traditional sense. You can still strive. You can still be ambitious. You can still want to win. But your *why* keeps you grounded. It protects you from the bitterness, envy, and self-doubt that can creep in when your focus drifts outside yourself, and it makes the journey infinitely more joyful.

NINETEEN

MOVING FORWARD

ONCE YOU'VE GROUNDED YOURSELF IN YOUR *why* and articulated your mission, the next step is applying that clarity to help you move forward, especially when fear, hesitation, or past mishaps want to pull you back. Let's say you're someone who wants to ride with presence and confidence, but maybe you had an accident as a result of a mistake. Or maybe something else rattled you. As a result, you're stuck. You keep replaying what went wrong.

Or let's say that you're continually second-guessing yourself at work, or doubting your ability in some other area of your life. Whatever the obstacle is, when your mind starts imposing self-limiting beliefs, it's time to take action.

This is where your *why* and your mission statement come into play. They are no longer abstract ideals, but real tools for navigating obstacles.

Here's what I see all the time in my work: People love to talk about obstacles. They'll say things like, "I can't move forward because..." or "This always happens when I try to improve." They become so entangled in the barrier that they can't see a way around it. It's as if they're riding straight toward a jump, eyes locked on the pole they're afraid to hit. And we all know what happens when you focus on the pole: You crash into it.

Instead, I encourage my clients to shift from being problem-focused to solution-oriented. It's not about denying challenges—injuries, fear, and frustration are real—but staying stuck in the narrative of what could go wrong only builds brittleness. It creates a mindset that can't bend or bounce back.

To move out of that fear loop, keep your eyes on the long game. Ask yourself: "Where do I want to go? What am I working toward?" Let that vision guide your decisions. Then ask yourself, "How can I work through this? What's the next step that keeps me aligned with my purpose?"

Mistakes happen—on course, at home, at work—and when they do, the people who stay grounded in their mission are the ones who recover, reset, and keep going. It's the difference between spiraling into "I ruined it!" and pausing to say, "Okay, that didn't go as planned—what now?"

Clarity of purpose rewires how we think. It doesn't only change what we do; it changes how we see and

approach challenges. When you're securely tethered to your *why*, setbacks feel less like failures and more like data. They are something to learn from rather than something to fear. You become less brittle and more resilient.

Resilience: Learning to Bounce

Resilience is the ability to *bounce*, not break. It's what allows you to ride through imperfection, parent through stress, lead a business through uncertainty, and keep showing up again and again.

Resilience is vital not only for performance, but also for your overall mental well-being. It's not something you achieve once and check off a list. Like physical fitness, resilience is something you build and maintain through daily practice. It's fluid. It adapts to the challenges of the moment.

Resilience isn't about being hard or emotionless. In fact, it's not the same as mental toughness. Mental toughness often implies pushing through at all costs, ignoring discomfort, or burying emotion. Resilience, on the other hand, allows for presence, flexibility, and recovery. It's about staying connected to yourself, especially when things get hard, and having the internal tools to respond rather than react.

True resilience is composed of skills like perspective-taking, emotional regulation, and self-compassion, all guided by a deeper awareness of your values and purpose. You don't power through the storm; you learn how to ride it with steadiness and grace.

Fortunately, resilience can be cultivated, and the more you practice it, the more it will show up for you when you need it most.

Perfectionism, by contrast, makes us brittle. It leads us to believe that if we make one mistake, we're finished. But real strength and true confidence come from our ability to absorb, adapt, and keep going. That's what we want to cultivate. That's what will carry you to your next level—not avoiding every misstep, but knowing who you are and why you're here, no matter what happens. Resilience starts with choosing to see the solution over the setback every single time.

Resilient individuals move through adversity with a kind of grounded energy that sets them apart. They're proactive rather than reactive, motivated by a sense of inner purpose rather than waiting for external pressure to push them forward. At the core of their resilience is something psychologists call an *internal locus of control*, which means they believe they have influence over their own lives, rather than blaming circumstances, luck, or other people when things go wrong. This mindset doesn't mean they control everything, but they take ownership of what they *can* control and act accordingly.

When opportunities arise, resilient people tend to seize them. They don't wait for perfect conditions. This quality doesn't come from ego or arrogance, but from a quiet confidence. It's an optimism that acknowledges setbacks but chooses not to be discouraged by them. Resilient individuals are invested in outcomes, but not consumed by them.

And here's something often overlooked: Resilient individuals generally have a great sense of humor. The ability to laugh at yourself, to find lightness in difficulty, is a deep sign of emotional strength. Humor helps us be resilient—to bounce back into shape.

Levity often partners with another underrated performance enhancer—joy. We want to find joy in the process and joy in the craft. Most people think success leads to joy, but I believe it's the other way around. Joy leads to *better performance*. Resilient people carry a kind of gratitude in their daily work; they approach life with humor—or, really, perspective—and joy.

These traits are supported by a set of practiced, trainable skills. One of the most important is the ability to manage focus—to turn it on when the moment calls for deep presence, and to turn it off when it's time to recover. Without that off switch, burnout creeps in. Another important skill is the ability to recognize, seek out, and receive support. Resilient people aren't lone wolves. They know when to lean on their circle, whether that's a coach, a psychologist, a teammate, a mentor, or a trusted friend. They don't confuse asking for help with weakness. They see it for what it is: wisdom.

Resilience isn't a superpower you're born with. It's a combination of qualities and skills that you can nurture, day by day. It's not about being bulletproof. It's about being equipped to show up fully even when things get tough.

When I work with my clients, whether one-on-one or in group seminars, I find myself coming back to this image again and again. You take a stumble—maybe in the ring, maybe in life—and instead of cracking or crumbling, you absorb the impact, spring back up, and keep moving. It's like being on a trampoline. The fall doesn't flatten you. It lifts you.

I help my clients cultivate the capacity to bounce. I want them to learn how to take the misstep, the awkward jump, the missed cue, the setback, and not let it define or derail them. Instead, we acknowledge it, learn from it, and then move on. Having a clearly defined *why* and a well-articulated personal mission statement helps you do this by giving you a destination and purpose to keep moving toward.

Stop the Self-Punishment

Unfortunately, many people, especially women, have an ingrained habit of self-punishment. I see this everywhere. It's buried in the way we talk about mistakes, in how we minimize our wins, in the stories we tell ourselves after a ride doesn't go exactly right. I see it in the posture, the tone, the looping narratives—and when I do, I aim to interrupt that cycle.

I ask, "Why are we punishing ourselves? Is it helping? Are we done yet?" That's the moment when we begin to rise.

My work is about lifting people up, getting them out of the muck, and helping them see the sky again. I remind them of where they're going, why they started, and who they're becoming. Once they reconnect to that bigger vision, they begin to bounce more easily. They don't fall quite as hard, and they recover faster.

They start to live like people who know their worth. They're striving, learning, and growing. They're in it for the long haul, and they've learned how to bounce.

As I often say, "Okay, you made a mistake. You're human. Join the rest of us." So you missed a distance, made a mistake or error of judgment? That's no reason to attack yourself. Stop replaying it. Allow yourself a bit of grace; learn from it and move on.

I had a client very recently who had a great day in the show ring. She won a big National Hunter Derby class on a new horse; it was a first win for this green horse. Then, in the next class, which was also a derby, she made an unplanned decision midcourse. She opted for a high-option jump she hadn't prepared for, aiming to earn that extra point. She got there on the half stride, the horse refused, and she was mortified. She kept saying, "It was so stupid. I can't believe I did that."

I told her what I tell so many others: "Okay, so you got overly competitive. That's all. You got greedy at that moment. That's part of being human. Everyone's been there. I've been there. We've all gotten overly competitive at some point and let it cloud our judgment. Even the greats make mistakes. You're not alone."

When you find yourself in a similar spiral, remember: Even the best riders in the world, like Boyd Martin or McLain Ward, make mistakes.

When you make a mistake, name it, normalize it, and then let it go. Carrying a mistake around like a bag of shame doesn't help you. It weighs you down.

I have this same struggle. Recently, something really got under my skin. I was in my workout class, a class I've been doing for years with my trainer. I love it. It's helped me get strong enough to ride my horses in the way that I want. I push myself hard. I don't do it to compete with anyone else. I do it for me because I know what I'm capable of, and I want to live up to that.

But in the middle of class, another woman teased, "Teacher's pet."

It hit a nerve. I've heard that line my whole life—since fourth grade, probably earlier—and it still stings. It also misses the point entirely. I'm not doing extra reps to get approval. I'm doing them because I want to be the strongest, most capable version of myself. That's my standard.

I didn't stop or say anything. I just kept going, but inside, I thought: *Don't say that to people. Especially not to women who are showing up and pushing themselves.*

Remember, when we lift each other up, we all rise.

There's another woman in that class who's incredibly strong and flexible. She can do these hopping moves that are unreal for someone in late middle age. I watch her and think, *That's amazing.* So I tell her, and then I try to emulate it. Her athleticism and drive inspire me.

That's the kind of energy I want to foster. Whether in the saddle, in a workout class, or anywhere else in life, we need to lift one another up. We need to let ourselves be inspired without shrinking in comparison.

If you've been stuck in self-punishment, consider this your invitation to stop. Let it go. You're not perfect. Neither am I. No one is perfect. But you're striving. You're learning. You're growing. And that's enough.

When Envy Rides Alongside You

I've thought about that "teacher's pet" comment probably more than I should have. Why did it bother me so much, and perhaps more importantly, why did that woman say it in the first place? Here's what I concluded.

Sometimes when we're in a group setting—whether it's a workout class, a riding clinic, or even scrolling social media—and we find ourselves muttering something sarcastic or dismissive under our breath, it's not really about the person we're targeting. It's a clue, like a flare fire from the deeper part of ourselves, saying, "Something inside me is feeling small."

Maybe it's insecurity, or maybe it's envy. Maybe it's fear that we're not doing enough or being enough. Those little biting thoughts and comments are messengers, and they're worth examining.

If I'm in a class and I catch myself thinking, *Ugh, teacher's pet,* I have to stop and ask: *Why do I feel the need to bring her down? What discomfort in me is surfacing right now? What unmet goal or hidden fear is bubbling up?*

When we diminish someone else's effort, we're also diminishing ourselves. In essence, we're giving ourselves permission to stay where we are. *Well, she's trying too hard anyway.* That kind of thinking lets us off the hook, and it also keeps us small.

One of the most beautiful and powerful things we can do is *choose* to admire others; we can emulate the best and be inspired instead of threatened. I think back to the woman in that same workout class who does those intricate hopping moves with such grace and power. Every time I see her, I celebrate it. I say, "Wow. That is amazing hopping. I want to emulate that." And I mean it. Her strength lifts me. My admiration of her lifts *both* of us.

That's the high road, and it's available to all of us, always.

Of course, I've experienced the flip side too. I've read books that triggered envy. I've watched others succeed and felt that familiar tug of competitiveness or inadequacy. But now I know that feeling is a signal pointing me toward something I care about.

> **Envy, when we meet it with curiosity instead of shame, can be clarifying. It says, "That matters to you." And the next question becomes "What are you going to do about it?"**

We can stay stuck, stewing in comparison and criticism, or we can take action. If we feel envy, channel it. Let it lift us instead of shrink us.

This practice of noticing our low-vibration reactions and choosing a higher one is at the heart of emotional growth. Again, it's about resonance and how we show up in our energy and presence. When we gossip, judge, or grumble under our breath, we're not just dimming others; we're dimming ourselves.

But when we admire, when we lift others up, when we lean into our discomfort and get curious about it, we rise, and everything in our lives gets better for it.

It never feels good when we're stuck in a place of smallness. You know the feeling: that inner curmudgeon who feels threatened by someone else's success, muttering critical thoughts under their breath, or silently shooting darts at people. Maybe this exists only inside your head, but still, it's there.

That kind of mindset makes us ill—emotionally, physically, energetically. It's draining. When we let ourselves sit in that bitter energy too long, we can actually feel it settle in our bodies. The joy drains out, and instead of being expansive and present, we start to shrink.

But when we celebrate others, even quietly...when we admire their strength, their grace, their hustle...then we feel that little spark. We feel that lightness and joy. It's subtle, and it's real. It's not just about being a good person. It's about feeling good and living in a way that elevates rather than diminishes.

So when those darker thoughts arise (and they will—remember, we're human!), it's an invitation to pause and reflect: *What's going on in me right now? Why am I feeling this way?* Sometimes we lash out at others because we're uncomfortable with something in ourselves.

That's why, when I tell stories like the one about being called "teacher's pet" in a fitness class, it's not just to laugh or vent. It's to show how these little moments offer powerful opportunities for self-awareness. How we show up in everyday life matters. When we feel the urge to diminish someone else, we need to ask ourselves: *What am I avoiding in me?*

KEY TAKEAWAYS

- Clarity of purpose rewires how you think. It doesn't just change what you do; it changes how you approach challenges. When you're securely tethered to your *why*, setbacks feel less like failures and more like data. They are something to learn from rather than something to fear. You become less brittle and more resilient.

- When we diminish someone else's effort, we're also diminishing ourselves. It's as if we're giving ourselves permission to stay where we are. That kind of thinking lets us off the hook, and it also keeps us small.

- Envy, when we meet it with curiosity instead of shame, can be clarifying. It says, "That matters to you." And the next question becomes "What are you going to do about it?" We can stay stuck, stewing in comparison and criticism, or we can take action. Channel it. Let it lift us instead of shrink us.

- One of the most beautiful and powerful things we can do is choose to admire others, to emulate the best, and to be inspired instead of threatened.

WRAPPING IT UP

There's much more to say about all the topics we've covered—trust me, that is what keeps me busy in the office! I know both personally and professionally that the emotional, mental, and psychological work continues—and changes—throughout our lives. We're never really "fully baked," as my grandmother would say. This psychological work is a practice, like working out. You don't expect to lift weights once and be strong forever. You build physical fitness by showing up over and over again, working on different aspects of yourself as you become fitter and stronger. It's the same with your emotional and psychological fitness.

You don't read one book, have one breakthrough, or attend one clinic and suddenly become perfectly resilient. Rather, you show up, reflect, realign, ride the highs, and learn from the lows. You create your own practice, whether that's through meditation, journaling, mindfulness, psychotherapy, or riding—or all of the above.

Even after years of inner work, including two full psychoanalyses, decades of study, and coaching hundreds of clients, I still do the work every single day. If I don't, I too slip into smallness and start to lose my shine. It's human. That's why we—you and I—must practice.

So, I hope this book is your invitation. Not to fix yourself, and certainly not to punish yourself, but to create a way of living that helps you stay aligned with your values, your joy, and your strength. Embrace your ambition and dare to say it out loud.

Remember, real transformation isn't found in perfection. It's found in your dedication to keep coming back to the work, again and again, and to help others do the same. That's where the magic lives.

I believe in you.

ACKNOWLEDGMENTS

There are so many people to acknowledge here that it's hard to know where to start! I guess I'll take my own advice and just start, knowing that all roads will lead to Rome.

I want to acknowledge all of the amazing and wonderful clients and patients I have worked with over my thirty-five-year career as a psychologist and performance coach. Thank you for trusting me with your stories—your grief, anxieties, and hopes and dreams. I am truly honored and humbled by your trust, and I have learned from each and every one of you. I hope you see some of yourself and our work in these pages.

I also want to thank all of the people who told me repeatedly that I "needed" to write my book and pushed me to do so. It was Julie Garella who finally shoved me off the diving board, but there were many other friends and colleagues standing by the side of the pool cheering me on. Phoebe Rubenstein,

Shabnam Behzadpour, Wendy Stern, Mary Steele, Elizabeth Simpson, Lisa Sobrero, Katherine Kennedy, Averill Pessin—you've all heard parts of this manuscript in one way or another. I deeply appreciate your support and encouragement. Thank you for seeing me and helping me hold the dream.

Thank you to Kristin Clark, Rennie Dyball, Kacy Wren, and the team at Cheval Press for making this manuscript a reality—and a beautiful one at that! I'm so grateful to you for holding the idea, lifting it up, and making it shine.

Thank you to my horse trainers and dear friends, Kylee Arbuckle Lorenzo and Heather Roades, for all your dedicated, loving support of me and my boys. The barn is my sanctuary, and you are the guardians of that sacred space and my beloved horses.

Thank you to Randi Merzon and Vivian Kushner for your guidance, healing, and love—always.

Thank you to my wonderful children, Peter, Adele, and Clara—you are the lights of my life, my pride and joy. I love you to infinity and beyond.

Last but most certainly not least, I want to acknowledge my husband of thirty-four years, Tom Bonomi. Thank you for always listening patiently to me, for being the absolute best cheerleader and my biggest fan. Thanks for keeping the vision big and always calling me out when I try to shrink. I love you forever.

About the Author

Darby Bonomi, PhD, is a sport and performance psychologist based in Marin County, California. Formerly a clinical psychologist and psychoanalyst, Dr. Bonomi shifted her practice in 2016 to focus on sport psychology and performance coaching. She currently works with amateur and professional athletes across the country, mainly competitive equestrians, along with entrepreneurs and young professionals starting their businesses. Almost all of her clients are women aiming to play bigger in their lives and to not shrink under their own self-criticism or that of others, or under their belief that somehow they are not enough.

Dr. Bonomi's writing has been featured in many magazines, including *Practical Horseman*, *USHJA In Stride*, *The Plaid Horse*, *Riding Magazine*, and *The Chronicle of the Horse*, among others. She has given performance psychology seminars throughout the United States. This is her first book. You can learn more about her and her work at *www.darbybonomi.com*.

www.ingramcontent.com/pod-product-compliance
Lightning Source LLC
Chambersburg PA
CBHW022105240926
51848CB00008B/62
* 9 7 8 1 9 6 7 5 0 9 1 0 2 *